In Their Own Words:
Stories of Healing & Practices for the Church

Doctor of Ministry Project
Lancaster Theological Seminary

Rev. Dr. Jason T. Link

Table of Contents

S0-BYX-164

Abstract

The purpose of this project was twofold: 1) to research how the church community can be a place of healing in people's lives, and 2) to suggest practices that when enacted would help a church to be a place of healing. Church life was differentiated into three levels: Pastorally, Relationally, and Congregationally. A group of people were interviewed who had received some type of healing and their lives and were asked to share how the church community helped in the healing process. Based off of the information gathered in the interviews, practices were suggested for the church at each of the three levels of church life.

Introduction

Jesus said, "I came that they may have life, and have it abundantly" (*NRSV* John 10:10). Yet life oftentimes brings with it diagnoses of cancer, children with disabilities, marriages that are breaking up or already broken. How can life be lived abundantly in the midst of the pain, struggles and difficulties of life? How can the church be a place where the message of abundant life is proclaimed? How can the church be a place of healing in people's lives?

As the pastor of a local church I have seen the pain, loss and suffering first hand. I have received the phone calls, I have sat and cried with people, I have held hands and prayed with people, I have been with couples and helped them talk to each other and not just past each other. I have seen pain, loss and suffering first hand.

I have also seen healing. I have been with the elderly man going in for surgery whose family is told that he probably will not come out alive, and yet surrounded by prayer and the grace of God, that elderly man is still with us and just a little bit older. I have counseled and prayed with a husband and father whose wife just left him and who has attacked his character in court and accused him of being a bad father. Through the healing process that husband and father is moving towards a place of hopeful resolution and healing.

Yet not everyone experiences or receives healing in the same way, or at all. I have talked with an older woman who lost her husband, and even though she felt that he was nothing more than a thorn in her side for the last 10 years, she now lives with feelings of guilt and depression. I have talked with a young girl who was sexually assaulted and has not had many restful nights of sleep since.

From what I have seen, heard and experienced, the church has the potential to be a place of healing in the lives of people. The message of the Gospel is a message of hope, healing, new and abundant life. Has the church forgotten this message? Is the church afraid to proclaim this message? Are the people not hearing this message? How can healing take place in the church today? What are people's experiences of healing? What keeps some people from experiencing or receiving healing? What does healing mean to someone battling cancer or struggling through a divorce? How can the church be a place of healing in people's lives?

This project explores how people talk about their own experience of healing, in their own words. What was it like to receive the diagnosis or the news? What was the process like as you progressed through the illness or struggle? What role, if any, did the church play in your experience? Would you say that God healed you, and in what ways were you healed? In what ways are you still not well or wounded? Listening to people share their own experiences would provide insight into how the church can more effectively and appropriately be a place of healing in people's lives.

Overview of Research Method & Process

The first part of this project involved interviewing a selected group of individuals. There were two rounds of interviews conducted with a total of seven individuals who had experienced some kind of healing in their lives. The scope of this project does not involve drawing statistical conclusions, but rather giving voice to the stories of a selected group of people who have experienced healing in their lives. The goal of this project was to give people the space and place to share openly about their experience of healing, and to help them give faithful language to their experience. Chapters Three, Four and Five share the stories of the people who were interviewed. Their names and some of the story details have been altered to protect their identity and some of the more private details. The goal was to capture *In Their Own Words* their experience of healing, and that is what hopefully comes through in the stories that are shared in chapters Three through Five.

The second part of this project was to take what was learned through the interviewing and to write about how the church was a place of healing in people's lives. Listening to the experiences of people and hearing how the church was helpful in their healing process provided insight into identifying specific approaches or practices that churches can undertake in their ministry to be a place of healing in peoples' lives. In chapters Six, Seven and Eight specific practices are outlined that directly reflect what the interviewees shared in their stories.

The structure of this project is built around the idea that church life happens at three basic levels. The first is described as Pastoral or through individual interaction or counseling with a pastor or other trained individual. The second is described as Relational or through small group experiences and relationships. The third is described as Congregational or through worship services and other whole church experiences. While the basic ideas that are shared in this project are not necessarily new and revolutionary, having this structure in mind as an individual church organizes a healing ministry will be very beneficial. From other resources encountered on healing in the church, I have not read any that use an organizational or structural model like this. Recognizing the different levels of church life and how they interact with one another will be of great benefit to a church that wants to begin or further a healing ministry. Each level is important to achieve an integrated and fully effective healing ministry at any given church.

Review of Important Literature

There is quite a wide variety of literature available today that speaks to many different understandings of healing. Some of the other literature I have read presents the healing process in an almost recipe like style: say this prayer, rub this oil, buy this cloth, and presto you are healed. Other literature teaches that you just need to have enough faith to be healed, and that if you have prayed for healing and have not received it you are just lacking in faith. Still other literature teaches that healings do not happen anymore, that healings were just a thing of the past.

Two sources more than any others have truly provided me with bookends to my own thinking on the topic of healing and wholeness – Epperly's *God's Touch* and Dawn's *Being Well When We're Ill*. Both Epperly and Dawn wrestle with the difficult, mysterious and challenging biblical texts that look at the healing process, while also sharing about the real life experiences of people today. A fuller discussion of the bookends that these two books present follows in chapter Two.

It is important in any study or research to understand the historical perspectives on the topic. Porterfield's *Healing in the History of Christianity* provides a look at how Jesus' healing ministry has been understood over the course of the last 2,000 years. Porterfield writes:

> Healing is a persistent theme in the history of Christianity, threading its way over time through ritual practice and theological belief, and across space through the sprawling, heterogeneous terrains of Christian community life and missionary activity. To focus on healing in the history of Christianity, as this book does, is to attend to important elements of continuity amid the jumble of competing doctrines, innumerable churches, disparate behaviors, and historical developments. (3)

Having knowledge of the differing understandings of Jesus' healing throughout the history of Christianity gives the researcher insight into how people today have been shaped and formed in their own understandings of healing. Porterfield provides a chapter on each of the major time periods of history, outlining the different understandings of Christian healings in these time periods as well as discussing other religious belief systems. Again from Porterfield:

> Christian healing can be distinguished from other forms of religious healing in its appeal to Christ as the transcendent source of healing and prime symbol of personal and

social integration. As a religious practice, Christian healing has involved many diverse actions including prayer, pilgrimage, penance, laying on of hands, participating in sacraments, and venerating saints, relics and icons. (9)

Having the knowledge of the historical spectrum of how healing was understood has provided me a much greater understanding of how people understand healing today.

Evans' *The Healing Church* also provides a much briefer overview of the how the church has understood and taught about Jesus' healing ministry as a way of introducing her main topic of how the church today can and should be involved in the healing ministry of Jesus. Evans writes:

The church's healing ministry can be divided into different periods that illustrate these emphases: (1) Jesus' healing ministry, the apostolic and patristic periods; (2) the founding of hospitals during the Middle Ages; (3) the medicine/religion split, starting with the Renaissance/Reformation; (4) the medical mission movement in the nineteenth century to mid-twentieth century; (5) the religion/medicine and bioethical quandary debates in the 1950s-70s; and more recently, (6) the development of health ministries. (2)

While Evans provides this brief history in the opening chapter, the real goal of her book is to write about how the church and the medical community can collaborate and coordinate to provide healing. This book provides a very holistic understanding of the healing process, recognizing the interconnectedness of science and religion. "In addition to health care's incorporation of spirituality into its delivery systems are the growing number of scientific studies that provide information about the impact of religious beliefs and practices on health" (43). Evans' book helped me to understand how the health care system and our own religious belief system can interact with each other.

Evans' *Healing Liturgies For the Seasons of Life* is a wonderful worship resource in which Evans compiles healing liturgies and prayers from a multitude of resources into one very highly organized volume.

> Understanding what healing means is central to planning a healing service. Healing is any activity that moves an individual or community toward "wholeness," a concept rooted in a Christian perspective of the integration of body, mind, and spirit with God at the center and the source of all healing. It is the affirmation of one's potential within the limits of the human condition. All are in the

permanent need of God's grace and therefore are in need of healing. (1)

Evans has brought together the healing liturgies of multiple denominations into one volume and organized them according to particular themes. Evans also provides an introduction to each theme to give the reader a fuller understanding of what is to come. As a pastor or worship team looks to develop healing services, Evans' book will prove to be very valuable. Evans writes in her Conclusion that:

> it is my hope that as the reader has studied and used these liturgies, an understanding of the depth and breadth of human need is present, as well as of the ways that pastoral care through worship is possible. I hope too that an appreciation of various Christian traditions may lead to the use of liturgies different from those of one's own denomination. While the language may be strange, it is often in fresh voices that God speaks to us – God's Spirit is never confined to our particular theologies. (451)

Epperly's *Healing Worship: Purpose & Practice* also provides some very helpful liturgies and prayers for healing services. Epperly's goal is to help the reader understand the purpose or reasoning behind the practice and application of healing worship.

> Jesus' healing ministry reminds us that divine healing arises not only from the interplay of our faith and God's desire for healing, but also from our appropriate use of a variety of complementary and Western medicines. Healthy theology is, above all, practical. It presents an integrative and life-affirming vision of reality; it tells people that they can experience the truths that it asserts; and it provides a pathway to lived experiences of theological doctrines. (15)

The liturgies and prayers are fully integrated into Epperly's writing so the reader can fully see and experience what he is writing about. The book includes a chapter entitled *The Healed Healer* in which Epperly stresses the need for pastors to take care of themselves in order to be effective in offering healing to others.

> Ministry is profoundly incarnational in nature. While there is power and effectiveness in the office of ministry and the sacraments of the Christian church, the primary medium of healing ministry is the pastor, her- or himself. Healthy pastors shape their congregations in healthy and

life-transforming ways. Unhealthy pastors
do the opposite! (99)

More so than any other book, this one has
provided the answers to the questions of why and
how as far as providing healthy, healing worship.
In a somewhat similar format, although
definitely intended more for individual use rather
than congregational settings, Norberg and
Webber's *Stretch Out Your Hand* provide a
wonderful book that presents an understanding of
the healing process, especially in relationship to
the act of prayer. "When we open the door to the
exploration of healing prayer, we find a
bewildering variety of theologies and styles in the
practice of the healing ministry today" (10). The
reader is invited to enter into their own experience
of healing prayer while reading the experiences of
others who share their own stories. Norberg and
Webber provide a very helpful chapter of answers
to *Frequently Asked Questions about Healing*. These
questions run the gamut from *Isn't it selfish to pray
for myself when other people are so much worse off?*
(36) to *Why are some people not healed?* (44). The
theology and understanding that Norberg and
Webber present is very much a hopeful
understanding of healing, full of possibility and
potential. "God desires our health, our wholeness
of body mind and spirit" (51).

Even when our lives are filled with suffering or wracked with agonizing questions, we can cling to the faith that God is with us, somehow always offering new life and healing. Not all healing will be physical, of course; often healing comes in emotional and spiritual realms where God's love is able to overcome every obstacle. (52)

My own understanding of the healing potential in our world is greatly influenced and informed by the writing of Norberg and Webber.

Lastly, two books written by medical doctors have provided insight into how science and theology, or as I will term them later in this project meditation and medication, can work together in the healing process. In Gills' *God's Prescription for Healing*, Gills discusses the full integration of how God has meticulously and careful created our bodies to be well and whole, and how physicians can come alongside patients and provide medical assistance to allow people to find the wellness and wholeness in their bodies. "The human body represents a scientific revelation of the presence and personality of an Intelligent Designer of great wisdom who loves and heals" (3). Gills discusses how doctors and health care professionals use the knowledge they possess to bring about healing, displaying a cooperation of scientific advance and our naturally integrative bodies.

When you are sick or injured, you turn for healing to those men and women who must do their job within their understanding of our created design. They examine, interpret tests, administer medication, and repair or alter with surgery. You anticipate their knowledge and skill to bring you comfort and relief – and to restore you. They employ techniques and apply scientific knowledge to reestablish the integrity of a body whose natural ability to defend or develop is enfeebled, broken down or nonexistent. They apply the techniques in line with the principles of nature, of the divine design of the body. (41)

It is important to recognize that our bodies are an amazing creation all in themselves, an amazing creation that God desires to be well. Having a medical understanding of what healing involves gives a broader and fuller understanding to the process of healing.

Dossey's *Healing Words* discusses in great detail the positive effects that prayer can have on people who are recovering from recent medical procedures. Studies have been done that sought to understand the effect of prayer on patients who were ill.

These studies showed clearly that prayer can take many forms. Results occurred not only when people prayed for explicit outcomes, but also when they prayed for nothing specific. Some studies, in fact, showed that a simple 'Thy will be done' approach was quantitatively more powerful than when specific results were held in the mind. In many experiments, a simple attitude of prayerful*ness* – an all-pervading sense of holiness and a feeling of empathy, caring and compassion for the entity in need – seemed to set the stage for healing. (xvii)

Dossey shares how when he was first introduced to these studies he was not sure what to make of them. However, over time he came to see the need to do further research on the topic.

My belief that prayer can and should be tested experimentally has resulted in large measure from my experience as a physician. It is simply a fact that patients sometimes improve dramatically following prayer; and in my judgment, when something affects human bodies, it becomes the legitimate concern of medicine to find out more about it –

scientifically, if possible – by asking
questions. (9)

The rest of Dossey's book is an exploration of
those questions and the answers that arise. It was
important to be aware of this research as I looked
at the responses that people gave during the
interviews, for prayer definitely had a positive
effect on those who shared their stories of healing.

These are the major sources that have
informed my understanding of the healing
process. Taken individually, they each present a
particular view or lens in which to understand the
healing process – historically, liturgically,
personally and medically. Taken all together, they
display an integration of all of these views or lenses
and gives a full picture of the healing process.

There are of course many other books on
healing available to today's readers. Each one will
present a particular understanding or view of
healing. Each one will either resonate or not with
the reader. I have found it valuable to read a
variety of views and understandings of healing, for
even the authors with whom I might disagree, I
come to see a new or different side of the healing
process.

Chapter 1 – Process (of) Healing

Big World

We live in a big world, a big world in which the possibilities for our lives are almost endless. I say almost, because there are certain limitations on our lives. For instance, at 6' 2" tall and more than 200 pounds, I will most likely never be a horse jockey. My height and weight create certain limitations for me, and also possibilities. If you have ever been at a high school or college graduation you almost certainly have heard someone say, "You can be anything you want to be." In reality, you can be almost anything you want to be. Being almost anything you want to be involves recognizing that we do live in a big world, a big world in which the possibilities for our lives are almost endless.

Possibilities abound in our world – possibilities for growth and learning, possibilities for development and nurture, possibilities for wholeness and healing. Jesus said in John's Gospel, "I have come that they may have life, and have it abundantly" (*NRSV*, John 10:10). The abundant life that Jesus gives to us is a life of possibilities, a life of opportunities, a life of wholeness and healing. Jesus didn't come to give us a "ho-hum" life, or a 50 percent enjoyable life. Jesus came to give us an "abundant" life, a life full of possibilities and opportunities, a life full of wholeness and healing.

Healing, Cure & Wholeness

The words healing, cure and wholeness can mean many different things to different people. Most often it seems that the delineating line between healing and cure is between the emotional or spiritual nature of a person and the physical nature of a person. To be cured is to no longer have the ill effects in one's physical body, while to be healed is viewed as coming to a new and better emotional or spiritual reality, with or without a cure. It is in this sense that we can talk of receiving a healing without receiving a cure. The opposite is also true, that someone can receive a cure, but never receive a healing in the sense that they are not able to see themselves or the world that they live in differently after being physically cured. The word wholeness often has a broader understanding to it, incorporating the physical as well as the emotional or spiritual side of people. How we think about and define these words can often create or limit the possibilities of the world in which we live.

I take a very holistic approach to my understanding of the words healing, cure, and wholeness. I believe healing can and does happen physically, emotionally, spiritually, financially, relationally – on all possible planes of our lives. Healing happens in our lives when we are open to the possibilities that our world presents on all these planes of our lives. Often healing happens on multiple planes all at the same time. I believe God's healing touch is multifaceted and multidimensional. God's healing is not limited to physical illness. God's healing touch can reach all aspects of our lives. A physical healing can also bring a spiritual healing; a spiritual healing can lead to a relational healing. The interconnected nature of our lives and the world in which we live in can lead to a ripple effect of healing in someone's life, where one healing sets off the possibility of a different healing, which can put into movement yet another kind of healing.

Due to the ripple effect within the healing process, I am not always comfortable with a strict distinction of the term cure being used to describe only the alleviation of physical symptoms of a disease or illness. Much research has been done to support the great interplay between physician prescribed plans of treatment and the offering of prayer to the one who is ill (Dossey 169-195; Gills 102-106). What the research shows is that people who were being prayed for while also undergoing a plan of treatment for their illness or disease got better quicker than those who were not being prayed for. Those who work in this field talk about this as complementary medicine, a working together of the medical field with those who believe in the positive power of prayer. I like to think of it as the cooperation of "meditation with medication".

However, I do think it is important to have some understanding of a differentiation between being cured physically, and being healed spiritually. For some people in our world, there is no physical cure for the disease or illness with which their bodies are afflicted. Think of people whose bodies have been invaded and affected by cancer. Even after they have gone through a treatment regimen of possibly surgeries, chemotherapy or radiation, and even after years of remission where no cancer has been found on tests and scans, doctors will very rarely if ever say someone is cured of cancer. And yet, I have met people who have been through surgeries and chemotherapy and radiation, who although they are not cured of the cancer that has affected their body, they are healed from that cancer. They have found a peace and a new way of living life in spite of the physical situation within their bodies. For some, a cure will bring a healing. For others, a cure will come but never healing. For still others, a cure will never come, and yet they are healed, made whole.

Finding wholeness in our lives is important for our spiritual and physical well being. Being physically ill, even with just the common cold, will impact and affect our lives emotionally, spiritually, relationally and in many other ways. In the same way of thinking, not feeling spiritually whole and connected to God will cause us to react differently on physical, emotional, and other planes within our lives. Finding wholeness, or a sense of balance and equilibrium in our lives, is important to our physical and spiritual health. Our interconnected selves seek and strive for that sense of wholeness, so that all the planes of our lives can be working in concert with each other, to create that balance and equilibrium, that feeling of wholeness.

The terms, healing, cure and wholeness are difficult, if not impossible, to fully define. The interplay between healing, cure and wholeness will look different for each person, depending upon what the circumstances are that they are involved with. Concrete definitions or defined expectations for what a healing, a cure, or wholeness looks like are not very helpful as each person will experience healing, cures and wholeness differently.

Each person's process of seeking wholeness and healing is unique to the individual. There are a number of factors that affect an individual's ability and willingness to receive healing and find wholeness for their life. There are no definite forms or patterns, no prescribed fail-proof methods, no certain and fully tested healing prayers. Healing is a process, a process that just like the world in which we live, the possibilities are almost endless. The healing process will look differently to different people. The path of healing will go in a variety of directions for a variety of people. The Good News for all people though, is that God intends for us to be whole and healed in our lives. God intends for all of us to live abundant and full lives.

Individual Response

It would not be an overstatement to say that each one of us is responsible in large part for our own sense of healing and wholeness, as well as the healing and wholeness experienced by other people. How we respond to God's movement and interaction in our lives, as well as how we respond to the movement and interaction of other people in our lives, will greatly influence the healing and wholeness we can experience. This is not the same as a "name-it and claim-it" kind of theology that fully places the burden of one's situation in life squarely on an individual's shoulders. The "name-it and claim-it" kind of theology has often been used almost as a club, telling people that if they just believed hard enough and prayed long enough, all will be well in their lives. The message that too often comes through is that they have not believed hard enough, or prayed long enough, and so God is punishing them. In contrast to that way of thinking, I want to affirm my belief in the need for people to seek healing and wholeness for their lives, but also for people to understand the interconnected nature of the world in which we live, interconnected with God, with nature, and with other people.

Process Theology

Much of my thinking on the subject of healing and wholeness has been greatly influenced by Process Theology, a stream of theology that sees the world as a place of almost endless opportunities and potentiality, where the natural world and created beings are deeply connected, and where the decisions people make can and do have an effect on other people and places far greater than we might ever imagine. We are the authors of the stories of our lives, and we help to write the story of other people's lives as well. We write the script for our lives, and we help to write the script for the lives of all the people with whom we interact. We live in a world in which we have choices for our lives, choices that will in big and small ways help to shape and determine the path that our lives and the lives of countless others will take.

We also live in a world that has limitations. Gravity, for example, limits objects from simply floating around in the air. Process Theology affirms both the possibilities and the limitations of our world and God's interaction within the possibilities and the limitations of our world. The world that God created is a very amazing world, a world with almost endless possibilities, a world where what some might call miracles are instead powerful workings of God, nature and humanity within the possibilities and limitations of our world.

Within this way of understanding how God interacts with us in our lives is also the understanding that the healing process is a give and take. We must be open and willing to receive the healing in whatever form it might come. The healing may be finding a way of coping with an illness or disease from which you may never be cured. A healing may only come when you allow yourself to be opened to a new way of looking at a particular relationship. Or a healing may only occur when there is death, and pain and suffering is over. The healing process involves a willingness to do our part to bring about the healing for our lives rather than just waiting for God to act. The healing process involves actively pursuing the healing and the wholeness for one's life.

Unfortunately for many, there are barriers that can sometimes keep them from receiving a healing for their lives. For some, this might be a resistance to say they were healed by God, but instead to put more faith and trust in doctors and medications than in God and the power of prayer. For others, their resistance may lie in the suspicion or stigma that many have towards the so called "faith-healers" we see on television and read about in newspapers. The sometimes magical or supernatural spectacle of what they claim to do may seem unrealistic and therefore cause some people to be suspicious of the whole idea that God can heal people. While I do not want to discount the work and ministry of faith-healers, nor do I want to downplay the importance of competent doctors and advances in medical procedures and medications. I also do not want to downplay the role that God has in creating skilled doctors and nurses, and giving researchers the abilities to develop new procedures and to create new medications. As previously stated, I want to affirm the positive interaction of both medication and meditation in the process of healing.

This positive interaction of medication and meditation is not hard to see in the interconnected and interrelated world in which we live. God is at work in our lives, the lives of people around us and the lives of people all around the world. God is also at work in the physical world around us in ways that we sometimes can recognize, but also in many ways that we never fully see. I like to use the example of how the internet is connected around our church office as a way of explaining that interconnected and interrelated world. Attached to my computer through a phone line and an Ethernet cable is a device called a wireless modem and router. It is through this device that I am able to access the internet to check my e-mail and surf the web. In the office next to mine there is another computer, but it only has a little USB antenna that sits on the desk and blinks that computer shade of green to show that it is active and connected. The wireless modem and router in my office communicates, or is connected to, that little USB antenna in the office next to mine, and allows that computer to access the internet as well.

All of us, whether we can recognize it or not, are hard wired to God, connected to God, just as that wireless modem and router are hard wired into my computer which allows me to be connected to the rest of the world. Sometimes we are able to sense or feel that we are connected to God, while other times that connectedness with God might not be so evident. All of us are connected to people that we know, and other people we will never meet face to face, in ways that sometimes we can see and understand, while other times those connections are a little harder to comprehend. This is how God's healing can take on the multidimensional and multifaceted possibilities of reaching all planes of our lives, in ways we can see and recognize, and also in ways that are not fully evident to us. God's healing in our lives does not have to be a supernatural event, for the natural world in which we live is full of possibilities and creativity. The natural world that surrounds us is pretty miraculous all on its own. God's healing takes place within the possibilities of what life presents.

Each situation of life presents the possibility for healing. There is not a definitive process of healing, for as stated earlier healing will look different for different people. The process of healing must be experienced by each individual in their own time and in their own way. Formulaic prayers or patterned procedures may actually do more harm than good for people seeking healing, for if those prayers or procedures do not bring about a sense of healing, people can be left with an even deeper sense of despair and hopelessness. The ways in which God will bring healing and wholeness to our lives may not always be what we expect or what we might wish for ourselves. Part of the healing process is remaining open to the ways in which God will move in our lives, and having a spirit of grateful receptivity to however and whatever God will do in our lives. We live in a world where possibilities abound and a lot should be anticipated from our creative and inspiring God, as well as from ourselves. God's energy is always flowing in our lives and in the world around us.

Part of the healing process is also being open to and aware of God's energy and God's desire that all people be well and be whole in their lives. Struggles and difficulties will affect all of our lives and it is important to remember that in the midst of the struggles and difficulties God will not abandon us. The struggles, difficulties and pain in our lives can have a redemptive effect on our lives when we are able to see God "even when we walk through the darkest valleys" of our lives (*NRSV*, Psalm 23:4). Not all healing will be perceived as positive life experiences, for healing can sometimes involve death. Healing for the terminally ill patient whose only prayer is to leave the pain and suffering of this life behind to receive the crown of righteousness that awaits them will look much differently than healing for the family members left behind to mourn the passing of that loved one.

Pain and suffering have always been a part of the tapestry of our world. However, God has also always been a part of the tapestry of our world. Part of God's message to the world is that pain and suffering do not have the final word, but instead God has entered into the pain and suffering of the world and conquered that pain and suffering with redemption. Jesus Christ offers us that redemption through the cross, and because of that we can receive healing in the midst of the pain and suffering of life. This is not to take away from the real hurt and loss that pain and suffering can bring, but instead to provide a message of hope in the midst of the struggles and difficulties that life can sometimes bring.

The church has the unique opportunity to be a place where this message of healing and wholeness can be proclaimed, and yet the church has often remained silent, not proclaiming this Good News. The message of the Gospel is a message of hope, healing and new and abundant life. Has the church forgotten this message? How can the church be a place of healing in people's lives? I want to challenge the church to lift up its healing voice, to celebrate the healing and wholeness that God offers us, to encourage people to share about their experiences of healing and wholeness.

In the next chapter we will explore a theology of healing as we look at two of the healing stories we have from the Gospels, as well as looking at two different authors' perspectives on the idea of healing. In the chapters that follow, we will read the stories of people who have experienced all varieties of healing within their own lives, and we will hear in their own words what that experience was like for them.

As a way of organizing this project and helping to see the different levels of church life, I have created three categories of Church Life: Pastoral, Relational and Congregational. We will look at the stories of healing through the lenses of those three areas of church life. In the concluding chapters, I will outline some practices for the church to implement in its life and ministry to create a place of healing for people. The goal in all of this is to empower the church to proclaim the message of abundant life and the message of healing and wholeness for all people.

Chapter 2 – A Healing Theology

A Choice

Even in a world of almost limitless possibilities, receiving a healing requires a choice, a choice of being open to the possibilities that healing presents, or a choice of being closed off to those possibilities. This is not the same as saying that an individual is solely responsible for whether he or she receives healing. There are some illnesses and diseases that are beyond a physical cure, some situations in life that may be too devastating from which to find any healing. There are however, many more diseases and illnesses in which a physical cure can be found, or instances of loss or suffering in life where healing can occur.

Jesus asks two questions in two different healing stories that I think provide a very good glimpse into Jesus' theology of healing, and also provide questions to ask ourselves as we create an understanding of our own theology of healing. The first is the question that Jesus asks the man who had been ill for 38 years that Jesus encounters by the pool in John 5.

> After this there was a festival of the Jews, and Jesus went up to Jerusalem. Now in Jerusalem by the Sheep Gate there is a pool, called in Hebrew Bethzatha, which has five porticoes. In these lay many

invalids – blind, lame, and paralyzed. One man was there who had been ill for thirty-eight years. When Jesus saw him lying there and knew that he had been there a long time, her said to him, "Do you want to be made well?" The sick man answered him, "Sir, I have no one to put me into the pool when the water is stirred up; and while I am making my way, someone else steps down ahead of me." Jesus said to him, "Stand up, take your mat and walk." At once the man was made well, and he took up his mat and began to walk. (*NRSV*, John 5:1-9)

Many who were lame, blind or paralyzed lay by the pool whose waters supposedly held healing powers. The first person to get into the pool when the waters were stirred would be healed. John tells us that this man who Jesus meets had been ill for 38 years – 38 years of waiting, 38 years of lying down, 38 years watching others get in the pool before him.

It would be interesting to know why Jesus singles out this man to offer him a cure and a healing. What was it about this man that drew Jesus' attention? Did Jesus know he had been lying there for 38 years? What we do know is that Jesus sees this man and asks him the question "Do you want to be made well?" Do you have a desire to be made well, whole, able to walk? Do you want to move beyond the place that you currently are in your life? As an observer of this story we may think the answer to Jesus' question is easy – of course this man wants to be made well. However, the man's response leads us to wonder if he does want to become well: "Sir, I have no one to put me into the pool when the water is stirred up; and while I am making my way, someone else steps down ahead of me."

I cannot say that I know what it is like to be paralyzed in any capacity for 38 years. I cannot say that I fully understand the range of emotions and feelings that this man had. What does seem clear from his answer is a sense of resignation, a lack of desire, a lack of will, a lack of wanting to move forward from where he is in his life to a new place. Jesus asks the question, "Do you want to be made well?" and the man responds by saying, "Well maybe, but I am not willing to do too much, or to try too hard. I have become comfortable in my illness." This paralyzed man has resigned himself to living on the sidelines of life. It seems that for this man his life has been 38 years of people waiting on him, 38 years of people taking pity upon him, 38 years of not moving forward in life. Maybe he has become comfortable with the paralysis that has damaged his body. What Jesus is prepared to offer this man is not only a physical cure, but also an emotional healing, a holistic change for his entire life.

There seems to be a lot of people in our world who are comfortable in their illness or disease, whether it is physical or emotional. People become resigned to the idea, and possibly also to the reality, that life will not or cannot get any different for them. People become comfortable holding on to the emotional scars of past hurts or wrongs, and they hold on to those scars never allowing themselves to be healed so they can move to a new place in their lives. People cling to the diagnosis of the doctors and limit their lives and the activities of their lives because of the fear of what might happen. People begin to enjoy the pity and sympathy that people give to them, and they feed off of that pity, never seeing a reason to be healed. People lay by the pool for 38 years, waiting for someone else to help them in, lamenting to Jesus that no one else will help them, never really wanting to be healed and made whole anyways.

A Resigned Theology of Healing

I would describe this way of viewing healing, as a resigned theology of healing. Dawn, a very well respected author and theologian has written a book about her own struggles with healing and wholeness that I think in many ways presents this resigned theology of healing. Dawn shares stories of healing, many of which come from her own life, and writes about healing occurring on multiple planes within her life. However even in the stories in which she talks about healing, there is never the sense that healing can happen in a full way. Dawn writes very early on in the book,

> This is a book, however, about losses that cannot be recovered. When severe or chronic illness or disability invades, we might lose our sight, our hearing, our physical strength or mobility, our mind. This book is not about those instances when these physical gifts can be restored by surgery or exercise. The losses might be delayed or somewhat softened, but there is no total cure. As my kidney transplant team often stressed, even a transplant is not a cure; it's a treatment. I'll be tied to immune-suppressants for the rest of my life, and these medicines themselves cause all sorts of damage. (1)

Dawn's book is written specifically for people, like herself, who have chronic illnesses or disabilities or for those who care for people with chronic illnesses or diseases.

For Dawn, and for others whose lives parallel the chronic suffering and disability that Dawn lives with each day, this resigned theology of healing may be a way of coping and dealing with life debilitating and life limiting illnesses. Dawn writes,

> The title of this book was carefully chosen. It does not claim that we can *feel* well when we are ill or disabled. It does not even claim that we can *do* well, for we might presently be in a state which prevents us from being able to do much of anything. Nonetheless, it is possible for us to BE well by the grace of God, for spiritual wellness is sheer divine gift. We will, though, receive the gift of wholeness more easily if we know about and are open to its treasures. (7)

Clearly for Dawn, a physical cure is not required for spiritual healing – "Emotional, intellectual, and spiritual wholeness don't require physical wellness" (7). Living life with chronic pain and suffering, as Dawn writes about it, is a day by day struggle in which life is lived resigned to the pain and suffering and yet also seeking something more.

This resigned theology of healing becomes even clearer in Dawn's discussion of the meaningless nature of chronic illness. Dawn writes,

> The worst problem with chronic illness and impairments is that they are often so meaningless. Furthermore, they dominate our lives so much that they render all of life

senseless. Truly, all is vanity. Calamity falls
upon us, and we feel snared in an endless
cycle of nonsense. (39)

There is a sense of hopelessness expressed here,
and maybe rightly so. Dawn continues by writing,

> Cancer is probably the most meaningless of
> chronic illnesses. It strikes willy-nilly. We all
> know too many people who followed all the
> rules for avoiding cancer and were hit by it
> nonetheless. One very dear friend of mine
> lived a calm but active life out in the
> farmland, didn't smoke, and ate only
> wholesome food – and not too much of it –
> yet she died at a young age from
> metastasized breast cancer. Vanity of
> vanities! (39)

While Dawn may question the meaning or
hope we can find in this life and the difficulties we
experience in this life, the meaning and hope that
she does cling to is in the life to come, that even
now we can experience. Towards the end of the
book, Dawn writes,

> As it turns out, then, our actual process of
> moving toward our physical death is much
> like all of life – daily we learn to die to
> ourselves so that we might live for God and
> His glory and for the sake of the world. We

are freed to do this because of our eschatology...As believers in the Triune God, we know that the work of Jesus brought the new aeon into the present, that God's culmination of His design for the universe has already been begun in Christ, that the Kingdom has already come, though it has not come fully. (232-233)

For those who suffer chronic illnesses and life debilitating disabilities, this resigned theology of healing may give them the strength to know that this life is not all that there is. Resigning oneself to what will be in this life may be the only way of coping in this life, while holding on to that hope that is to come. Finding times of peace and solace from the life altering pain and life debilitating diseases may be the only form of healing or wholeness that some can ever hope to experience.

A Hope-full Theology of Healing

There is of course another way of looking at healing, what I would call a hope-full theology of healing, a theology of healing in which the answer to Jesus' question, "Do you want to be made well?" would be an excited and exuberant "Yes!" Epperly, another well respected author and theologian, presents this hope-full theology of healing in his book (*God's Touch*). From beginning to end, what

Epperly writes about is the positive and life giving possibilities of healing that are presented to each one of us in a variety of forms. Epperly writes, "In contrast to those who limit God's healing to a particular type of medicine or form of prayer, I believe that wherever there is healing, God is present, by whatever name or technique the healing is invoked" (*God's Touch* 38). Each chapter works its way through some of the healing stories we find in the Gospels and shares how God has continued that work of healing in the lives of people today. Epperly writes about healing on a multi-level scale – through chemotherapy and prayer, through direct touch and channeled energy, through deliberate breathing exercises and through physical activity. The message that comes through without question from Epperly's writing is a message of a hope-full theology of healing.

Epperly's hope-full theology of healing is very much influenced by Process Theology and the interaction that exists between us and God as we seek healing. Epperly writes,

> From this perspective we can discern the interplay of divine and human power in every healing encounter. While the mechanics of healing will always remain somewhat mysterious, I believe we can assert a divine-human partnership or

synergy in every transformative event.
(*God's Touch* 44)

This interplay between us and God will create new opportunities and possibilities in our lives, opportunities and possibilities for new things to happen in our lives. The new things are not always well received, for as Epperly writes,

> Healing is always to some degree counter-cultural, for healing means seeing our lives differently, awakening to new talents, saying no to limiting visions of ourselves, whether they come from the church or temple, the physician, the prognosis for our illness, or from caregiving persons whose own stability depends upon our weakness and dependence. (*God's Touch* 64)

Each moment in life presents us with new opportunities for healing, or as Epperly writes, "In every moment of life, God is presenting us with an image of who we can be in that particular moment and that particular setting" (*God's Touch* 65).

This hope-full theology of healing even sees the healing possibility and potentiality in the midst of what appears to be life limiting or disabling situations. Epperly writes,

> God's transformation always calls us to experience the many dimensions of every

life – to become *creative non-conformists* who are not limited by our diagnosis or health condition, but who discover wondrous possibilities even within profound limitations. (*God's Touch* 95)

Epperly continues by writing,

As the source of our hope, God's touch challenges self-limiting concepts and life-destroying prognoses and social attitudes. God's touch invites us to boldly claim the possibility of personal transformation and healing for ourselves and others, despite the social and medical stigmas of illness. (*God's Touch* 96)

Saying Yes

It is this hope-full theology of healing that leads to the second question that Jesus asks that gives us a great insight into his own theology of healing. This second question is the question that Jesus asks blind Bartimaeus in Mark 10, "What do you want me to do for you?"

They came to Jericho. As Jesus and his disciples and a large crowd were leaving Jericho, Bartimaeus son of Timaeus, a blind beggar, was sitting by the roadside. When he heard that it was Jesus of Nazareth, he began to shout and say, "Jesus, Son of David, have mercy on me!" Many sternly ordered him to be quiet, but he cried out even more loudly, "Son of David, have mercy upon me!" Jesus stood still and said, "Call him here." And they called the blind man, saying to him, "Take heart; get up, he is calling you." So throwing off his cloak, he sprang up and came to Jesus. Then Jesus said to him, "What do you want me to do for you?" The blind man said to him, "My teacher, let me see again." Jesus said to him, "Go; your faith has made you well." Immediately he regained his sight and followed him on the way. (*NRSV*, Mark 10:46-52)

The healing of blind Bartimaeus is a pretty dramatic story. Jesus is just walking along with his disciples and a crowd, and as they are walking they happen to come across Bartimaeus, lying down, begging by the side of the road. Bartimaeus hears that it is Jesus who is walking by, and Bartimaeus starts shouting out to Jesus. The crowds tell Bartimaeus to keep quiet, to not bother Jesus, but Mark tells us that this only makes Bartimaeus shout and yell all the louder.

Jesus hears Bartimaeus calling to him, and tells the crowd to bring Bartimaeus to him, and so they do. When Bartimaeus is brought to Jesus, Jesus asks him that question, "What do you want me to do for you?" Without hesitation Bartimaeus responds to Jesus, "My teacher, let me see again." Bartimaeus knew what he wanted from Jesus, he knew what he wanted Jesus to do for him – he wanted to see again. For Bartimaeus receiving his sight would mean more than just the ability to see again, receiving his sight would involve a whole new world of opportunities being opened to him. Bartimaeus wouldn't have to beg anymore; he could go and get a job. Bartimaeus wouldn't have to lie on the side of the road anymore; he could build himself a house. Bartimaeus wouldn't have to be dependent upon other people anymore; he could now be the one to help others. Bartimaeus knew what he wanted Jesus to do for him, and he wasn't afraid to ask Jesus for it.

It seems to me that if Jesus was to ask Bartimaeus the question he asked the man at the pool, "Do you want to be made well?" Bartimaeus' answer would have been a resounding "Yes!" And on the flip side, if Jesus were to ask the man at the pool the question he asked Bartimaeus, "What do you want me to do for you?" the man at the pool might have just said, "I don't want you to do anything for me, I am fine just the way I am." To what extent are you willing to go in search of your healing? To what degree are you willing to make your desires known to God? How great is your desire to be healed and made whole? The answers to these questions and to Jesus' questions will greatly determine if one falls into the category of a resigned theology of healing or a hope-full theology of healing.

Healing as a Process

As stated before, I think there are people who have become very comfortable living within a resigned theology of healing for their lives. They have become so accustomed to their way of life, no matter how debilitating, physically or emotionally, that way of life is, that they lack any desire to receive the healing and wholeness that God offers to them. This is not in any way to diminish the real pain and hurt that experiences in life can and do have on our lives. However, for the well-being of our minds and bodies, we all need to find ways of moving beyond and moving forward from those negative experiences so we can live lives that are fulfilling and healthy.

There is also the danger of moving forward too quickly in the healing process, not giving oneself adequate time and space to grieve and process the real emotions that a loss or illness will bring. Rushing the healing process and not taking adequate time and space to grieve could lead to feelings of regret or remorse later on in life. When someone experiences loss, suffering or illness they will also experience feelings and emotions that need to be processed and worked through. Often times working through these emotions and feelings is best done through conversations with others who can be trusted and with whom we have a comfortable relationship. Just as the healing process will look differently for different people, the grieving process will also look differently for different people. It is important to honor and respect the grieving process even as we seek to help people within the healing process.

Jesus' Theology of Healing

If as I have suggested, Jesus' two questions provide us a glimpse of Jesus' theology of healing, what we can learn is that first Jesus wants us to be well, and secondly that it is important for us to ask God for healing in our lives. Jesus heals and cures both the man at the pool and blind Bartimaeus, inviting the man at the pool to stand up, take his mat and walk, while simply telling Bartimaeus to go for his faith has made him well, and immediately Bartimaeus was able to see again. Jesus wants us to be well, even if as in the case of the man at the pool, we are not fully sure we want to be well. In the end though, the man at the pool discovers and seizes the new opportunity that Jesus gives him by having the faith to actually pick up his mat and walk, moving beyond his resigned nature to imagine what could be. What Jesus wants for us is to be bold in asking for our healing, just as Bartimaeus was bold in getting the attention of Jesus, yelling over the crowd so he could make his request known to Jesus.

Jesus' theology of healing would be the hope-full theology of healing, a theology of healing where possibilities and opportunities abound, where healing and wholeness happen on multiple planes of our lives. For some of those whom Jesus healed, they were healed without any response of faith at all, much like the man at the pool. For others like Bartimaeus we are told that the healing was because of their expression of faith. This again displays the point that healing will happen differently for different people, that healing looks different for different people. What we can say for all people though, is that God wants us all to be well and whole, healed in our minds and bodies, our souls and our spirits. To receive all of the healing that God desires for us, we must be active participants with God, actively seeking our healing, openly making our requests for healing made known to God.

Living Healing

In my own life, I have adopted a practical way of living into the desire that God has for my life that I be well, and also my need to ask God for healing in possibly fractured relationships. If I sense that something I said to someone may have been received in a way that was not intended, I will begin with prayer to discern how best to respond to this situation. Oftentimes I have found that a phone call or e-mail, first offering my apology and asking for forgiveness, and then offering my explanation can diffuse what could have become a very volatile situation. I am aware that God does not want me or the other person to be burdened by the situation, and so I try to handle these situations sensitively and also timely, so that I and the other can again find wholeness in our lives.

In much the same way, when I have been offended by someone, I seek the Spirit's guidance and wisdom as to the words to say or write to express my thoughts and feelings in a way that will hopefully be received in a healing manner. I oftentimes will apologize and ask forgiveness for anything I have said that may have caused them to respond to me in a way that I found offensive, and to let them know I mean them no harm but only want them to know how their words were received. I have found that misunderstandings can be cleared up and situations can be resolved when the goal is not about being right, but instead seeking wholeness for both parties involved.

When it is a chronic physical illness that someone is suffering with, understanding how God desires for them to be well can be difficult. If God wants us all to be well, why doesn't God just cure all the sick people that fill the hospitals every day? If God wants us all to be well, why doesn't God provide us a cure for cancer? If God wants us all to be well, why doesn't God make our bodies more resistant to all the things that can go wrong in them?

While I am not sure there are really answers to any of those questions, I think an important aspect of one's healing theology needs to be a willingness to accept the things that are in life. We cannot fully control all that will happen to us in life. We cannot fully control whether we will get cancer, or have heart issues, or when we will die. We cannot fully control the experiences – good or bad – that we will have in our lives. What we can learn to do though, is to accept the experiences of our lives, the disappointments of our lives, the celebrations of our lives. Learning to find the healing and wholeness that God desires for our lives involves at some level accepting what is in life, and in the midst of that still receiving God's healing and wholeness.

The story of my grandmother's short battle with pancreatic cancer demonstrates this well. My grandmother, who was a nurse, had not been feeling well for quite some time. I think she knew something was wrong, and it wasn't a little something. Eventually the pain was too much and the doctor's diagnosis confirmed that something was wrong – it was pancreatic cancer. There were some other issues as well, a weakened heart and some digestive issues, and they would have to be worked on first. My grandmother contemplated surgery and chemotherapy, whatever treatment the doctor might suggest. There were a lot of discussions and consultations, and the best guess was that "if" the surgery was successful, and "if" my grandmother was strong enough for chemotherapy, and "if" her body responded well, she might live another six months. My grandmother accepted what was, she accepted that this was not something she would be cured from. Instead, she sought to find some healing in not going to these extreme measures, but instead getting well enough to go home and enjoy whatever time she had left surrounded by her family and friends. Sometimes being well, means leaving well-enough alone, accepting what it is.

My theology of healing is informed by all of these aspects – 1) God's desire that we be well; 2) the need on our part to pursue and name the healing we want for our lives; 3) the need to not rush the grieving process but to see grieving as part of healing; 4) to be willing to accept what is in life and still seek healing and wholeness no matter what the situation is. My theology of healing is a hope-full theology of healing; a theology of healing that believes in the full possibilities and opportunities that God desires for us as we seek healing and wholeness for our lives.

We will turn now to the stories of healing, told by those who have received healing in their lives. These are stories of regular people, real life stories, real life reflections and thoughts on what the healing process was like for them. We will hear about their theology of healing and where God was and was not in the midst of their healing. Their stories will illustrate how the church was helpful to them in their healing process. Most of all though, we will hopefully learn from them what the path of healing looked liked, that we too can find healing and wholeness for our lives as well.

Chapter 3 – Stories of Healing: Pastorally

The next three chapters introduce the stories of people who have experienced healing in their lives. In an effort to protect their identity, their names have been changed and some details of their stories have been omitted. In this chapter we will hear how people experienced healing Pastorally, or through one to one interaction with their pastor or other trained individual. Let's listen to their stories.

Prayer

For most people it was just another Tuesday morning. For Sue it was the day of her surgery. The diagnosis had been given – it was cancer, and the course of treatment had been prescribed – surgery and then chemotherapy. No one wants to hear the diagnosis of cancer, but especially not Sue, because her mother had died of cancer. The doctors felt they caught it early enough, and with the aggressive course of treatment they had prescribed things would be okay. Sue spoke about how "worry wasn't going to make it any better, I had to put trust in the doctors and in God."

Sue's surgery was scheduled for first thing in the morning that Tuesday, and so at about 5:30 a.m., Sue and her husband Frank got into the car and made the trip to the hospital. It was an uneventful drive that morning, and when they got there they reported to the proper floor and were taken into a hospital room. Papers were filled out, preparations for the surgery were worked on, nurses and doctors floated in and out of that hospital room where Sue was waiting. And then someone else walked into the room – Sue and Frank's pastor. Their pastor had made the trip just to be with Sue and Frank and to pray with them before surgery.

The same pastor was there early on a different morning when Frank was in the hospital to have a procedure done on his heart. It was another early morning for Frank and Sue, another early morning trip to the hospital. Frank had been very tired and weak, and the doctors said it was his heart. They could do a procedure that would get Frank's heart back into rhythm and give him his strength and energy back. Another 5:30 a.m. trip to the hospital, reporting to the proper floor and being assigned a room. Papers to be filled out, preparations for the procedure and doctors and nurse floating in and out of the room – Frank and Sue knew the routine. And then in the doorway was that pastor again, arriving in the early morning just to be with and to pray with Frank and Sue.

The next day Frank was still in the hospital. Things had not gone quite as smoothly as they had hoped and Frank was in a lot of pain. That pastor made the journey to the hospital again to pray and be with Frank and Sue. Sue talked about how the pastor showed up at just the time when they needed him most. Frank was in bed, obviously very uncomfortable. Sue had just taken a short walk to stretch her legs. When Sue arrived back in the room and she and Frank and their pastor prayed, it was much like a weight being lifted. Things were not magically and instantly better for Frank, but there was definitely a sense that things were going to work out. And things did work out for both Frank and Sue. Both have recovered very well and are enjoying now, maybe more than ever, their life together.

Lisa's story is much different, and yet there is a thread that connects her story to the stories of Frank and Sue. Lisa's mother was ill and in the hospital, it all happened very quickly. However, Lisa's mother had been given a second chance at life, or as Lisa talks about it, "it was like we had been given a gift, and we were." Breathing troubles had plagued Lisa's mother for many years and had gotten to the point that her lungs and her heart just could not keep up anymore. Lisa talked about how "one of the things I prayed about over the years was that it wouldn't be difficult for her." Thankfully it was not a long struggle for Lisa's mother, just four days in the hospital. It was a blessing for the family that they could all be gathered together during the last hours of Lisa's mother's life.

The next day, Lisa called her pastor and shared the news. The pastor expressed condolences and offered to help in any way he could. Lisa asked if her pastor could officiate at the funeral service and if they could have the service at their church, since Lisa's parents didn't have a church home. The pastor agreed and set up a time to gather with the family to talk about the service. When that time came, the pastor and Lisa's family gathered and they talked and shared stories. They talked about hymns for the service and special Scripture passages. And then they also prayed together. Lisa talked about how helpful her pastor's response was and how much she appreciated his willingness to be with and to pray with her and her family.

Interlude: Mark 5:21-43

When Jesus had again crossed over by boat to the other side of the lake, a large crowd gathered around him while he was by the lake. Then one of the synagogue rulers, named Jairus, came there. Seeing Jesus, he fell at his feet and pleaded earnestly with him, "My little daughter is dying. Please come and put your hands on her so that she will be healed and live." So Jesus went with him.
A large crowd followed and pressed around him. And a woman was there who had been subject to bleeding for twelve years. She had suffered a great deal under the care of

many doctors and had spent all she had, yet instead of getting better she grew worse. When she heard about Jesus, she came up behind him in the crowd and touched his cloak, because she thought, "If I just touch his clothes, I will be healed." Immediately her bleeding stopped and she felt in her body that she was freed from her suffering.

At once Jesus realized that power had gone out from him. He turned around in the crowd and asked, "Who touched my clothes?"

"You see the people crowding against you," his disciples answered, "and yet you can ask, 'Who touched me?'"

But Jesus kept looking around to see who had done it. Then the woman, knowing what had happened to her, came and fell at his feet and, trembling with fear, told him the whole truth. He said to her, "Daughter, your faith has healed you. Go in peace and be freed from your suffering."

While Jesus was still speaking, some men came from the house of Jairus, the synagogue ruler. "Your daughter is dead," they said. "Why bother the teacher any further?"

Ignoring what they said, Jesus told the synagogue ruler, "Don't be afraid; just believe."

He did not let anyone follow him except Peter, James and John the brother of James. When they came to the home of the synagogue ruler, Jesus saw a commotion, with people crying and wailing loudly. He went in and said to them, "Why all this commotion and wailing? The child is not dead but asleep." But they laughed at him. After he put them all out, he took the child's father and mother and the disciples who were with him, and went in where the child was. He took her by the hand and said to her, "Talitha koum!" (which means, "Little girl, I say to you, get up!"). Immediately the girl stood up and walked around (she was twelve years old). At this they were completely astonished. He gave strict orders not to let anyone know about this, and told them to give her something to eat. (*NRSV*, Mark 5:21-43)

What wonderful stories. There is the story of Jairus' twelve year old daughter who is ill, and also the story of the woman who had been ill for twelve years. As is often the case in stories of illness that we read in the Bible, we are not sure what the illness is that has affected Jairus' daughter, but the fear is that this illness will bring her to her death. Maybe a fever, maybe she ate some bad food, maybe she was bitten by a snake. In reality the exact illness doesn't really matter.

What matters is that Jairus has done all that he can do to help his little daughter. Jairus is a leader in the synagogue, and surely he has called upon the other leaders of the synagogue to do what they could for his daughter but nothing has worked. Jairus is down to his last resorts, to call upon Jesus to come and pray for his daughter.

Calling the pastor to come and pray can sometimes be the last resort for people today as well. The story of Jairus' daughter is interrupted by that other story, that other story of healing for the woman who had been ill for twelve years. We will return to her story in a moment. When Jesus arrives at Jairus' home, the mourning and crying had already begun for they believed Jairus' daughter had already died. The Good News for Jairus is that when Jesus is involved in the situations in our lives, things are not always how they appear.

Jesus empties the house, takes Jairus' daughter by the hand, prays for her, and "immediately the girl got up and began to walk" (*NRSV*, Mark 5:42). The words that Jesus prayed were not somehow magical or supernatural. What Jesus teaches us is that there is power in prayer and that prayer can cause things to happen, even if what happens isn't exactly what we wanted or were believing would happen. For Jairus and his daughter, prayer brought about healing and wholeness. Prayer caused life to be made new again for Jairus' daughter.

Prayer is not the only way for people to experience healing and wholeness in their lives. Sometimes, all that is needed is presence. That was the case for the woman who had been ill for those twelve long years. She had tried everything, and "endured much under many physicians" (*NRSV*, Mark 5:26). This illness had affected her life long enough; she too was at her last resort. "If I but touch his clothes, I will be made well" (*NRSV*, Mark 5:28). The woman believed that just being in Jesus' presence and touching his clothes would be enough to bring her healing and wholeness and she was right. Just as with Jairus' daughter, immediately after having the encounter with Jesus she was made well and healed. Being present, physically being with someone, can bring healing to their lives.

Presence

Before Tim and his now pastor and friend first met, they only knew each other at a cursory level, just enough to say hello or wave to each other as they passed one another while walking or driving. However, their relationship would become something much greater when Tim's wife decided one day that she didn't love him anymore and made up her mind to leave behind the home that they had made over the last ten years. Tim needed to turn somewhere for help, for guidance, for a listening ear. Tim decided to turn to the pastor of the local church right up the road from his house.

That pastor just happened to be on vacation that week, but was still in town, and so when he received the phone call from Tim, could sense the urgency in his voice and set up a time to meet that afternoon. More than anything else, it seemed that Tim wanted and needed someone just to listen. Tim wanted and needed someone just to be present in his life as he tried to process what had just taken place in his life. Tim wanted and needed someone to just sit with and have a conversation with.

"It was a difficult situation, unexpected, because we had four children" Tim shared. "I was the man, I had to fix the problems and make the marriage work." Tim and his pastor did work on it, talking about a whole host of issues and topics, but in the end the relationship between Tim and his wife was beyond reconciling. Tim and his pastor would get together at least once a week just to talk, just to be together, just to check in with each other. One thing that Tim's pastor was very clear about was that he did not have a magic formula or an instant fix for what Tim was struggling with. There was not a fool proof answer to the questions and issues that Tim was working through. What Tim's pastor could and did offer was his presence. There were times when Tim and his pastor would get together and Tim's pastor would offer words of advice or suggestions on how to handle a situation.

There were other times though, when all that Tim needed at that point was just to be in a room with another person who would just listen.

Jane was in a much different place in her life. As a teenager, Jane struggled with issues related to her image and her weight. Jane's pastor tried to be present in her life as she struggled with those deep issues during her teenage years, but by Jane's own words "I wasn't looking for help at that time." Now as a young adult who has made major strides in the battles of her life, Jane reflects back and sees how her pastor was trying to help by offering to meet and talk with her.

For Barbara the issue wasn't so much that she didn't want pastoral support and visitation, as much as it was centered on not having a good relationship with her pastor. Barbara was very active and influential in the church. There were a couple of times where Barbara's pastor had disagreed with something Barbara wanted to do or a change that Barbara wanted to create, and that had caused a lot of discord between Barbara and her pastor. When Barbara was diagnosed with cancer she turned to her pastor for support, and her pastor was there for her. Barbara and her pastor were able to reconcile and forgave each other. The presence of Barbara's pastor in her life meant a great deal to Barbara as she progressed through her treatments and recovery. Unfortunately, Barbara's cancer returned and would eventually claim her life. However, even in her last days, Barbara requested that her pastor come and be with her and pray with her. That pastor displayed his concern for Barbara by simply being willing to be present with her in her time of need.

Teaching

For Mary it was a sermon that her pastor preached that helped her through the healing process of her life. Mary's pastor was preaching about the story of the Healing of the Man at the Pool (John 5:1-9), and specifically the question that Jesus asks, "What do you want me to do for you?" Mary's road had been a long one. Diagnosed with cancer, the doctors felt that they could perform a surgery to remove all the cancer and all would be okay for her. A mammogram a few weeks after the first surgery indicated that the cancer had exploded and Mary was in for a second surgery the very next day. And then a year later, there was a third surgery. Mary shared that "at that point I did start to fear a little, not the cancer, but the doctor."

Two years later, Mary sat in church and her pastor was preaching and asked that question that Jesus asks, "What do you want me to do for you?" Mary's pastor asked that question of the people in the pews, "What do you want Jesus to do for you?" Mary shared how she knew what she wanted Jesus to do for her – "I want Jesus to cleanse me, and I want Jesus to tell me what he wants me to do in my life."

Mary had grown up in the church and the teaching of that church had given her a rock solid base for her life. Mary shared how she "had been brought up in the church, the church that introduced me to God, and taught me that God will take care of me and that God will provide. And God did and I thank him every day. I had that base underneath me." The teaching and preaching that Mary had received over the years helped her in the healing process as it not only provided her a base from which to stand upon in her understanding of who God is, but also helped her in the midst of her recovery to name what it was that she wanted from God in the midst of her healing process.

We Need Other People

One of the most basic principles of our existence is that God created us to live with other people. We were not created to just go through life and figure things out and overcome difficult situations in our lives all by ourselves. We need other people, to pray with us, to be present with us, to help teach us. The pastor is certainly not the only person who can fulfill this role in people's lives, but as these stories display, the pastor is oftentimes the one to whom people come. In our next chapter we will explore the significance of the other relationships that people have and how those relationships can bring healing and hope to people's lives.

Chapter 4 – Stories of Healing: Relationally

The relationships that we have in our lives are very important to our overall well-being. We as humans were not created to live in isolation, but instead God created us to be in relationships – with other people and with him. Of the three areas I studied in people's stories of healing – Pastorally, Relationally, Congregationally – the relational aspect was by far what people talked about most. The relationships people had, and the importance of those relationships, had a very large impact on the stories people told about their experience of healing. In this chapter we will hear more stories of healing, and specifically how Relationally, or through interactions with other people, the process of healing was experienced.

Visits, Phone Calls & Conversation

Barbara, who we first met in the last chapter, was very glad to be able to come back to her own home after her cancer surgery. It had been a long week in the hospital and the familiarity of home would be a good thing, not to mention being able to sleep in her own bed again. Even though Barbara certainly was tired from her stay in the hospital, she very much appreciated the visits that people made to her home, just to say hello and wish her well. "It was nice when people came to the house to visit. It made me feel connected to the larger community. And no one stayed too long – I think they recognized I still needed my rest even though I was feeling much better," Barbara shared.

For Sue who was recovering from her recent surgery to remove the cancer from her body, phone calls were important too – "the biggest surprise was all the phone calls, people calling just to see how I was doing." Sometimes it did get to be too much, and there were times when Sue wanted to take the phone off the hook. And for Lisa who had just lost her mother, it was just ordinary conversation that helped her through the healing process. Lisa shared how "it was helpful to have conversation with family and friends who have also lost loved ones." Maintaining normal interaction and feeling connected to their friends were all a part of the healing process for Sue, Barbara and Lisa.

Basic Human Kindness

Tim experienced the relational aspect of healing in a much different way. There was some apprehension on Tim's part concerning how people would treat and respond to him after the separation from his wife. Would people treat him the same, or would things now be somehow different? Would people look down on Tim because of what took place in his life? Tim was almost overwhelmed with the "common courtesy and concern" that people expressed. Tim also shared that those in his community of faith were "helpful in their good heartedness." For Tim these positive healing experiences with other people enveloped more people than just his close friends: "There are some very good people who I only know at a cursory level, but the way they have treated me and my family really resonates with me."

Frank, who was recovering from heart surgery, echoed much of the same that Tim experienced. Frank shared:

> The concern that people had was overwhelming. People who you didn't even know knew there was something wrong coming up and asking how you were doing. It's amazing – down at church we don't know all the people real well – for those kind of people to really show concern is overwhelming.

For Frank though it wasn't just people from church. His neighbors were a great source of healing as well, helping with stuff around the house and yard, helping with whatever Frank needed help with. For Lisa, it was just simply "people's sincere expressions of sympathy and sorrow – it was all very helpful."

Feeling Supported

Lisa also shared about having the community supporting her, "knowing that the church was supporting me even if words were not spoken." Just knowing that other people knew of her loss and were concerned for her following the loss of her mother provided her the ability to begin the healing process. For Barbara the experience was much the same. Barbara was a member of several church and community groups. She shares of how "within each one of those groups, I had a tremendous amount of support." Spoken or unspoken – the support was felt by both Lisa and Barbara.

For Jane, who struggled with issues related to her weight and image, the support was there, but was only recognized as she looks back on the situation. Jane wasn't looking for support from her faith community but instead was trying to do it all by herself. Looking back now she can say "I absolutely believe that the support and encouragement from the church was a pivotal part for me." Mary's story is similar in that she "didn't tell the church about her diagnosis of cancer, but the church did help me without anyone knowing it." People may never fully know how or to what extent the support and encouragement that they offer will be felt and experienced by those who are in the healing process.

For Sue the support came in a different way. Sue shared how on the in-between weeks of chemotherapy treatments two of her good friends "would come and take me out to lunch, they didn't miss one. I knew they would be there to take me out to lunch. That meant so much knowing that they were going to be there to take me out to lunch." In another story involving meals, Sue shared how "people from church would bring a meal to the house on the days I had chemotherapy. It was a long day for Frank and I. One day someone from church brought the meal, and I said 'Thank you,' as I walked her to the door. But she turned to me and said, "No, thank you for letting us do something to help because we so feel so helpless to know what we can do."" Part of the healing process is not only receiving the support from others, but also allowing others to express their support to those in the healing process.

Interlude: Mark 2:1-12

> A few days later, when Jesus again entered Capernaum, the people heard that he had come home. So many gathered that there was no room left, not even outside the door, and he preached the word to them. Some men came, bringing to him a paralytic, carried by four of them. Since they could not get him to Jesus because of the crowd, they made an opening in the

roof above Jesus and, after digging through it, lowered the mat the paralyzed man was lying on. When Jesus saw their faith, he said to the paralytic, "Son, your sins are forgiven."

Now some teachers of the law were sitting there, thinking to themselves, "Why does this fellow talk like that? He's blaspheming! Who can forgive sins but God alone?" Immediately Jesus knew in his spirit that this was what they were thinking in their hearts, and he said to them, "Why are you thinking these things? Which is easier: to say to the paralytic, 'Your sins are forgiven,' or to say, 'Get up, take your mat and walk'? But that you may know that the Son of Man has authority on earth to forgive sins" he said to the paralytic, "I tell you, get up, take your mat and go home." He got up, took his mat and walked out in full view of them all. This amazed everyone and they praised God, saying, "We have never seen anything like this!" (*NRSV*, Mark 2:1-12)

What friends this man had! What faith they had! What perseverance they had! What a difference this group of friends made in the life of their paralyzed friend. How long had this man been paralyzed? How long had he been dependent upon his friends to carry him from place to place? I wonder if he even wanted to be carried to that home where Jesus was that day. I am sure he was thankful for his friends after hearing the words that Jesus would speak to him that day, the healing that he would receive that day. It would truly be an amazing day for him, but also for all who were there that day.

The crowd was so big that the man's friends could not get to the front door, but that was not going to stop them from bringing their friend to Jesus. They maneuvered through the crowd, pushed and shoved a little bit for sure, making their way to the roof top. Can you think of someone in your life for whom you would be willing to climb on a roof? I wonder what the owner of that house was thinking when those friends began to take apart the roof and eventually make a whole big enough to lower their friend down to Jesus.

Healing can sometimes be a tricky thing, something that not everybody will appreciate. The scribes objected to Jesus' first offering of healing, the healing and forgiveness of the man's sins. The scribes did not fully know who this Jesus is, for they said that only God can forgive sins. Jesus can not only forgive sins, he can tell a man to "get up, take your mat and walk" (*NRSV* Mark 2:11). Immediately the once paralyzed man stood up and walked out of the house, no longer carried by his friends, but certainly forever grateful to those friends.

What an amazing story of support and encouragement, a story that displays the healing potential that our relationships with other people will have. We may never know the reach or the extent to which our lives will impact the lives of those with whom we have relationships.

Cards

When I visited with Barbara after she returned home from her surgery to remove the cancer from her body, she still had the most recent of the cards she had received displayed on her windowsill. "I have received so many cards" Barbara shared, "I cherish each one." Sue also had cards displayed in her home. Sue was most amazed by "the one person from church who sent a card every week, every week like clockwork I knew I was going to have a card from her. It took time to go shopping and get the card and write it...and every week."

For Lisa it wasn't so much the number of cards she received, but instead "that I am still receiving cards six weeks after the death of my mother. I am amazed that people are still thinking of me and the loss I experienced. It really lets me know people still care." Frank, too, was amazed at all the cards he received, and from all the people he received them. "I received cards from people I never would have expected," Frank shared.

Prayers

Frank had a similar experience with people praying for him that the surgery to correct his heart rhythm issues would be a success: "I had some good people praying for me, people you wouldn't even think of. You just do not realize how many people are concerned for you, and let you know that they are concerned for you." Sue shared the same thoughts: "There were just so many people praying for you, you just have no idea the number of people praying for you. I was even on the prayer list over at the Catholic church!"

Barbara shared how "the prayers that many people offered for me were very, very helpful. There were times I could feel the warmth and caring from their prayers. Even though I have recovered from my surgery, people are still praying for my recovery and I am grateful." Even though Mary initially kept her illness quiet and did not share it with the community, word still somehow got out. Mary shared of how "people would say, 'I know you don't think I know but I do and I am praying for you.'" Mary felt a sense of calm and peace in knowing that she was being prayed for.

Relationships Matter

The relationships we are involved with in our lives matter, and may just be the single most important part of the healing process. Hopefully by hearing these stories you can see the value and importance of being in meaningful relationships for the general well being of your life. Having a relational circle that will offer you support and encouragement will also be very valuable in the face of loss or difficulty in life. As these stories illustrate, one's faith community can provide at least part of that relational circle.

In the next chapter we move to people's experiences of healing at the congregational level, and how through whole congregation experiences healing can happen. This will then give us a picture of how healing can happen at all three levels of life within a faith community.

Chapter 5 – Stories of Healing: Congregationally

What is the value of being a part of a community of faith for someone who has suffered a loss and who has entered into the healing process? That is the main question of the congregational aspect of healing. How was the whole church helpful to the individual in the healing process? What congregational aspects and activities helped people along the road of healing? The following are stories that answer those questions.

Responsive

"To an extent the people of the church didn't have an opportunity to help me because I didn't tell everyone. It got out through a few people and that was okay," Mary shared. The church was responsive to Mary, but Mary also wanted to guard her privacy, and did not want a big to-do made over her as she was battling cancer. "Knowing the people of the church were there and the depth of their faith and love for me did help a lot," Mary commented. It is very important for the church to be responsive to the needs of people while also not overstepping their welcome and becoming intrusive.

For Lisa, the experience was much different. Many in the church knew Lisa's mother, and also knew the struggle and difficulty of losing a parent. "When Linda (a member of Lisa's church) called, that meant the world to me." Lisa shared, "I definitely think the church was helpful." Lisa did not feel smothered at all by the phone calls she received: "I think sometimes people just don't know what to say when they call or see you. For me, just saying 'I'm sorry' or 'I have been thinking of you' was enough to know that people truly cared."

Supportive

Not only were people responsive to Lisa, she could also feel the support of people from the church – "just feeling the support, knowing that people in the church do care made the whole situation better." Sometimes that meant that words did not even have to be spoken. Lisa had learned from her time at her church that the people genuinely did care for those who were suffering a loss.

Tim's support from the church came in a much different way. Too often it seems that people are all too anxious and willing to try and fix the problem that others are having. Tim shared that "no one tried to fix the problem. Even when they gave advice it wasn't as, 'this is what you should do', but instead, 'this is what I have run into in my experience.'" Knowing how much help and support to offer can be a tricky balancing act of wanting to show support, while also not wanting to smother people.

For Frank, he has been able to pass on the support and advice he received to other husbands who are supporting their wives through an illness or loss. "I am now able to sympathize and talk with other husbands whose wives are also going through the treatments for cancer" Frank shared. Frank's experience at his church was truly an all around positive one. "The whole experience when we were ill, all of the three levels of church life – you can't say enough good about it." Sue echoes those thoughts and also adds she "doesn't know how people do it who don't have a church family behind them." The church family can provide a much needed level of responsiveness and supportiveness to those who are in the healing process.

Interlude: Mark 6:53-56

> When they crossed over, they came to land at Gennesaret and moored the boat. When they got out of the boat, people at once recognized him, and rushed about the whole region and began to bring the sick on mats to wherever they heard he was. And wherever he went, into villages or cities or farms, they laid the sick in the marketplaces, and begged him that they might touch even the fringe of his cloak;

and all who touched it were healed. (*NRSV*, Mark 6:53-56)

There are several similar stories in the New Testament of the multitudes being healed by the hands or cloak of Jesus. Jesus was a wanted man. Wherever he went the crowds followed him. It must have been exhausting for Jesus, but never once in these stories do we hear Jesus complain about the crowds coming to him. It must have been wearying at times, all the people, all the time, all their sickness, all wanting Jesus' healing touch. Jesus never sends them away, instead Jesus is always responsive to their needs, always supportive in offering them healing.

There must have been something comforting about going to Jesus as a group. People can oftentimes gain support and encouragement when they are together in a group. Jesus certainly cared for each individual, and was responsive to their individual needs, but Jesus also recognized that so many in the world in which he lived were in need of healing for their lives. Jesus offered that healing and so much more.

We need the support and encouragement of one another to make it through the difficult and devastating events of our lives. We need the support and encouragement of people around us to give us the strength we need when we are weak, to offer us hope when we feel hopeless. The crowds that came to Jesus all came looking for healing. They came as a source of support and encouragement for each other. They came as a community looking for healing. They left as a community filled with healing and hope.

It might seem a little like the question of which came first, the chicken or the egg, but sometimes I think we can get mixed up in believing that we as individuals exist for the community, where in reality it seems that the community exists for the individual. A community is a group of individuals that gathers together for a common goal or purpose. A church community gathers together for worship, prayer, service, support and encouragement. All of these activities are not meant to be done in isolation, but instead they are to be done in the midst of a community. It is in that sense that the community exists for the individual. The community exists as that place where individuals can come to worship, pray, serve and to receive and offer support and encouragement. The community exists as that place where we are called and invited to sometimes look past ourselves to see what we can offer to others, to see how we can be responsive and supportive to others in that community.

In a world that teaches and leads us to believe that each one of us is the center of the universe, it can be a humbling and sobering idea that we do not exist for ourselves, but instead we exist for others. We exist not solely for our own benefit or to fulfill our own desire, but we exist for others. We exist to be responsive and supportive and encouraging to others. The more we are able to recognize that for our lives, the more we will be able to offer words and actions of healing and hope.

Place of Sanctuary

For many, the church building itself provides a place of solace and comfort in the midst of whatever they are going through in their lives. Just entering the four walls of the church can have a positive effect on people's lives. That was certainly the case for Tim, who would regularly travel to the Catholic church in town, whose doors were open twenty-four hours a day. Tim shared how when he needed to just go and process all that was happening during his separation and divorce, he would go to the Catholic church and "sit in the pews, walk up and down the aisle – talking, asking questions, begging for knowledge and forgiveness." The church provided that place of sanctuary, that place of quiet, that place of the Holy that Tim was looking for in his life.

For others the experience of their home church can be too close for comfort and bring up too many sad memories of a recent loss. Lisa shared how "it was too hard to come to church – the memories are too fresh from the funeral for my mother." For Lisa and for others as well, the feeling will subside, and the church will become again that place of the holy, that place that centers our lives. Lisa shared how now "I have a hard time sitting in church in the aftermath of a loss. In the coming months it will help me to be there – it helps to ground me, bring me back, gives me that nourishment when I feel like I'm empty." For Lisa, "Sunday worship service is a time to just quiet your heart and allow yourself to focus on thoughts about where you are with the whole process."

Being a Part – Feeling Connected

What seems most important to people who are involved in the life of a local congregation is that they feel a part of that community and feel connected to those within that community. Gone are the days when people would move into a new town and immediately seek out the church of the same denomination from which they had been a part of in their old town. What matters is being a part of and feeling connected to the community of faith. It won't take a visitor very long to figure out whether they are welcomed and made to feel a part of any given community of faith. When people gain that sense of connectedness and being a part of the community of faith, the people of that community of faith can provide very valuable support and responsiveness when people in that community of faith experience loss or illness in their lives. Ultimately, the community of faith can be a place of sanctuary, the place to experience the holy, the place where individuals can feel connected to something bigger than themselves. They can feel connected to other people and to God, and that can only help in the healing process.

Chapter 6 – Practices for the Church: Pastorally

There is no "one size fits all" process or practice for pastoral ministry. The specific context, the cultural influences, the size and age of a congregation, as well as many other factors will create possibilities and limitations for any given congregation. With that being said, what I propose in the next three chapters are practices that any church can learn from and implement in its ministry to better create a place of healing within the lives of the people who worship in and serve from that congregation.

One of the things that hopefully you noticed in the three chapters in which we looked at people's stories of healing was how all three layers of church life influence each other and overlap each other. As we look to the practices that a church can be involved with to create a place of healing, we will see the same thing. To truly create a place of healing, all three levels (Pastoral, Relational, and Congregational) must be working together. As the children's song says, "You can't have one without the other."

Pray for Healing

Joe had gone into the hospital in need of a heart valve replacement. At the young age of 89, the doctors thought that he was a good candidate for this surgery, and that having this heart valve replaced would provide Joe with many more good years of life. The surgery went well and Joe was seemingly recovering well. However something went awry. Joe's kidneys were not functioning properly. The doctors discovered that Joe was allergic to the dye that they had used to color Joe's blood for the surgery. Initially what the doctors said was that Joe would need to be on kidney dialysis for the rest of his life because of this allergic reaction and the damage that was done to his kidneys. Joe was devastated. Kidney dialysis can be a very difficult treatment to receive and causes a lot of unpleasant side effects with which to live.

I had gone and prayed with Joe before his surgery, and prayed for a successful surgery. I prayed for the doctors and nurses, that they would have great skill and understanding as they operated on Joe. I prayed for God's healing hands to be upon Joe to bring him a good and whole life after the surgery. When I went to visit with Joe after the surgery and heard the news of needed kidney dialysis, I prayed with Joe again. I prayed that somehow the doctor's initial diagnosis would be wrong, that they had read the reports wrong. I prayed that God would intervene in Joe's life and that he would not have to be on kidney dialysis for the rest of his life. I went to church on Sunday and invited the whole congregation to pray for Joe, to pray for something to happen that the kidney dialysis would not be necessary.

God heard those prayers, and answered in a positive and life giving way, for when I went to the hospital to visit with Joe again, he shared the news that he would not need to have kidney dialysis at all. God hears all of our prayers, whether we receive the answer we would like to receive or not. One of the most difficult things in life is when we pray and we do not receive that answer. We may question whether God did hear us. We may wonder if prayer really does matter. The promise of God is that he will hear us when we pray, and that he will answer us, even if that answer is not what we were hoping for. God's possibilities for our lives are oftentimes much greater than we could ever imagine and the answer to our prayers may come in a very unexpected way. The answer to our prayers may come in providing a new opportunity that we might never have imagined, but an opportunity that God will provide. The doctors couldn't explain what had happened, but for some reason Joe's kidneys started functioning properly again. I cannot tell you exactly what happened either, but what I can tell you is that I prayed for Joe and Joe's congregation prayed for Joe, and healing happened.

One of the things I encourage pastors to do is to go and pray with people. Go to the hospital, go to the nursing homes, go to people's homes and pray. Pray with people before they go in for surgery, pray for people when they are at nursing homes, pray for people who are at home. And be specific in what you are praying for. Healing can look very different in different situations. Pray for a successful surgery with pain free days ahead. Pray that something would change in the doctor's reports and kidney dialysis would not need to take place. Pray that a job would come. Pray that marital issues could be resolved. Pray that God would allow someone to slip away quietly and peacefully into his loving arms. We also need to recognize that sometimes we may not like the answer that God provides to our prayers. God might lead our lives to unfold in ways that we do not want or wish for. God is not a genie in a bottle that we just rub and receive our wishes. Instead, God is the one who loves us and knows and provides what is best for us, as we cooperate with him in our healing process and the healing process for others.

I also encourage pastors to pray for people by name in the congregational setting. This is not to take away at all the fact that God knows the prayers of hearts even before we speak them, but instead serves as a reminder for us, to remember the names of those within the community who are in need. We are much more able to remember the names of those in need of prayer, when we have heard their names spoken aloud.

Elam was prayed for many times over the years, his name said aloud as the congregation prayed for him. Elam, 91 years young, would need those prayers again. Elam had fallen and banged his head, but had not told anyone. Eventually the pain and the headaches became too much and he told his kids. They took him to the hospital and the news from the CT-scan was not good. There was a blood clot on his brain. If they did not do surgery he would certainly die. If they did do surgery there was a very high likelihood he would die on the operating table. The family decided to go ahead with the surgery.

Prayers were offered, for Elam and for the doctors and nurses, and off he went to the operating room. The hours ticked by on the clock and then finally the doctors emerged. Elam had made it through the surgery, overcoming what seemed like impossible odds. Elam would recover well and enjoy many more years in his life. Elam's name was lifted up to God in prayer many times, by many people. God heard those prayers and God answered those prayers in life giving and sustaining ways for Elam.

Interlude: James 5:13-15

Pastors need to pray for the healing of the people whom they serve. God will hear those prayers, and while he may not always answer those prayers in exactly the way that we might think or hope, God will answer them. This is more than just helpful advice, but something we are instructed to do:

Are any among you suffering? They should pray. Are any cheerful? They should sing songs of praise. Are any among you sick? They should call for the elders of the church and have them pray over them, anointing them with oil in the name of the Lord. The prayer of faith will save the sick, and the Lord will raise them up. (*NRSV*, James 5:13-15)

When Jesus sent out his disciples, he sent them out with the power to heal. As disciples of Jesus today, Jesus sends us out with the same power – to offer prayer for the healing of the people. God desires for all people to be well, and so it is only natural that God desires us to pray for healing for the people who are ill and who have experienced a loss in their lives. In creating a place where healing can occur, the practice of praying for healing, individually with people as well as corporately during worship, will help to create an environment where people feel that they can bring their concerns and needs to be prayed for as well. When this happens, through the power of prayer, healing can begin to happen.

Teach about Healing

Another practice that pastor's should be engaged with as they seek to create a place of healing is to preach and teach about the many healing stories within the Bible. There are healing stories throughout the Bible, from Genesis to Revelation, and almost every other book in-between. The healing stories of the Bible are not limited just to Jesus, but healing occurs at the hands of many of the characters we meet in the Bible. When pastors take the opportunity to preach and teach about healing, they can open a whole new world to the people who will hopefully see that healing is not something that just took place in biblical times, but that healing can take place in their lives today as well.

One of the things I did a couple years back was to preach a 15 week Sermon Series on some of Jesus' healing stories (see appendix A). I think one of the most important aspects of teaching and preaching about healing is to introduce and share the idea that healing is more than physical or medical. Healing can and does take place spiritually, emotionally, financially, relationally, as well as physically. The healing process can touch all areas or planes of our lives, and the stories of healing that we have in the Bible describe that great variety and depth of healing.

A church could also offer a study group on healing, during which people can share their own stories and experiences of healing. When I have done this in the past, it is a very freeing experience for people because they hear from others who have also experienced healing, and sharing their experiences gives voice to their own stories and experiences. A church could also offer a Sunday School Class or other study class in which the participants read through a book together about the healing process or others stories of healing. The relational aspect of learning and studying together can really create healthy relationships within people from the church, one of the most helpful parts of the healing process as we heard from stories of those whom I interviewed.

A third idea of how to get people talking and sharing about healing, is to have a scheduled time when people can get together to share about and discuss their ideas about the healing stories we have in the Bible. For example, the following passage from Matthew's Gospel:

> Jesus left there and went along the Sea of Galilee. Then he went up on a mountainside and sat down. Great crowds came to him, bringing the lame, the blind, the crippled, the mute and many others, and laid them at his feet; and Jesus healed them. The people were amazed when they saw the mute speaking, the crippled walking and the blind seeing. And they praised the God of Israel. (*NRSV*, Matthew 15:29-31)

After reading this passage, the conversation could begin by simply asking, "What do you make of this story?" The leader could ask what people see in the story, what sticks out to them, what makes them wonder or question, what they cannot comprehend. The conversation could then flow in a multitude of directions, based on the experiences and ideas that people share. The goal is simply to present the idea of healing and to have people share their own ideas, questions, stories as well as questions and doubts. Many of the healing stories in the Bible are pretty amazing stories, unbelievable stories some might say. However, we certainly worship and serve an amazing and sometimes unbelievable God!

A fourth idea would be for a church to invite people who have experienced healing to share of their experiences or to give testimonials with the whole community. The pastor could certainly share the story for the individual if they do not feel they could share with the whole community, but first hand experiences of healing often have a very deep and moving affect on those who hear those stories. The whole community can be strengthened by hearing of the struggles, but more importantly the victory that people encounter in their lives.

Create Healing Relationships

One of the issues for pastors as they relate to the congregation that they serve is the pastoral boundaries that they will set and how they will relate to the people that he or she serves. There are some who feel that a pastor should not have any close friends within the congregation that he or she serves, that the pastor should only have professional, and by that it seems that they mean distant and removed relationships with the people within the congregation. Fear of abuse and of overstepping the right and safe boundaries of pastoral relationships with people within the congregation have caused this reaction. I wonder if some have reacted too strongly, and because of that we run the risk of creating too large of a chasm between pastor and church member. I appreciate healthy boundaries and think they are necessary for both pastor and member, but I also am very much aware that there needs to be a sense of closeness and relationship between the pastor and members, if the pastor is ever going to be able to help the member through the healing process.

A significant goal of the pastor is to create healthy, healing relationships with those whom he or she serves, relationships built on respect, concern, and care for those who he or she serves. To create healing relationships, the pastor must be willing to become a part of the life of the one who has come in need of healing. Creating healing relationships involves the pastor praying, listening, and sometimes just being with the one who has come seeking healing. These healing relationships can be formed at any time with people from the congregation, and actually it is far better to form them before a crisis or loss happens, so that individuals know that they can turn to the pastor for help and support and healing. There needs to be closeness within these healing relationships so that people feel comfortable coming to the pastor in their time of struggle and need. The people of any given congregation need to feel comfortable coming and talking with the pastor, if the pastor is going to be able to help in the healing process.

The Pastor as the Healing Hands of God

One of the images I love most is the image of God's hands, and how each follower of God is called to be God's hands in the world in which we live. It is such a powerful and yet simple expression of how God calls each one of us to use the hands that he has given us, as expression of his hands in the world around us. Pastors are those who are called in a unique way to be God's hands to a particular flock of people. It is a privilege and a responsibility to be God's hands to the people.

God's hands are powerful tools. Pastors as God's hands to a particular congregation have the potential to bring out goodness and healing. What God desires is for his churches to be healthy and whole and to be filled with people who are healthy and whole, inviting others to be healthy and whole as well. Pastors are given the privilege and responsibility to be the hands of God, and to bring about the goodness and healing and wholeness that God desires. Pastors are given the unique privilege and responsibility to pray for healing and to teach about healing and to create healing relationships with the people with whom they worship and serve. When a pastor is faithful to that privilege and relationship, pastors can help to create a whole community of healing.

Chapter 7 – Practices for the Church: Relationally

Almost any child who has been through Sunday School has learned the little song:

> I am the church, you are the church, we are the church together. All of God's children, all around the world – Yes we're the church together. The church is not the steeple, the church is not a building, the church is the people. I am the church, you are the church, we are the church together. All of God's children, all around the world – Yes we're the church together.

The church is the people, the people gathered together to worship, to serve, to fellowship, and to be a support and encouragement to each other. As was discussed in the Stories of Healing: Relationally chapter, the relationships that people had with others and the support and encouragement that they felt, was the single most important factor in people's stories of healing. The church can help create a place where relationships flourish, and people can be connected to each other in meaningful ways so that when people are in the midst of difficult situations in life they have a place and people to whom they can turn.

In a world where people are longing and searching for meaningful relationships, the church can create the place and help to facilitate those meaningful relationships. The church can teach the importance of good relationships as healthy ways of being connected to others in supportive and encouraging friendships. As we heard from the stories of those who were interviewed, it was the relationships that people had with others that meant the most to them. If the church can help create a safe place where relationships can be formed and strengthened, the church can be an integral part in the healing process for its members.

Community Formation Groups

One of the best ways for a church to be a place where healthy relationships are formed, is to encourage the formation of Small Groups within the church. At the church I serve, we call these groups Community Formation Groups. These are groups of five to twenty people that gather together around a common goal or interest. We have the Penningtonville Posse (a men's group), the Pearls (a sewing and crafting group), Kid's Club (a group for 2nd – 7th graders), Prayer Group (title says it all), and many others. These groups gather together in a community to encourage, support and help form one another, while also building meaningful relationships with one another. It is the people within a Community Formation Group that people most often turn to in the midst of a difficult situation.

We have built into our Mission and Vision Statements the value and importance of Community Formation Groups. Our Mission Statement provides direction for us as a congregation:

Helping people grow in their relationship to God through Worship,
Community Formation Groups, and
Mission & Outreach Opportunities

Our Vision Statement helps to flesh out our

Mission Statement:
Worship is a time to Come & Learn
Community Formation Groups are places to Share & Grow
Mission & Outreach Opportunities are ways to Go & Serve

In our Discipleship Process we continue to describe the importance of each of these three steps:

The Discipleship Process of Penningtonville Church involves inviting people to Come & Learn about who God is and who we are in relationship to God in Worship. The next step in the Discipleship Process is becoming a part of one of the Community Formation

Groups, in which individuals are connected to a group who are gathered to Share & Grow in their faith journey. We continue to develop as disciples as we seek ways of becoming involved in Mission & Outreach Opportunities. Mission & Outreach Opportunities provide us with ways to Go & Serve in a variety of different places using a variety of different gifts. The Discipleship Process never ends, but rather continues to evolve as we as disciples continue to Come & Learn in Worship; as we continue to Share & Grow in Community Formation Groups; and as we continue to Go & Serve through Mission & Outreach Opportunities.

For Penningtonville Church (www.penningtonvillechurch.org), Community Formation Groups are an integral part of our communal life together as a church. These groups can be formed around any variety of shared interests or goals – Bible Study, Prayer, work group, Mom's group, Senior Citizen's group, single's group – the possibilities are almost endless. The goal is to create a place where a small group of five to twenty people can connect with each other and feel supported and encouraged by each other. I have been amazed at how important these groups are to people's lives. Sometimes these Community Formation Groups will bring together people in meaningful ways that may have never happened if they had not been connected through the Community Formation Group.

The most successful Community Formation Groups at Penningtonville are the ones that have formed very organically, beginning as a couple people gathering around a common goal or purpose and then growing as others join in with the group. If the leaders of a church can do their part in identifying possible leaders within the church and suggesting that they lead a Community Formation Group, the church can go a long way in helping to create these opportunities for significant relationships to be formed.

Give People the Tools

One of the most common things that people will say in the face of a natural disaster is, "I want to help, but I just don't know how." I think that is also a common response that people have when someone they know has experienced a loss or an illness – they are just not sure what to do. People want to help in the healing process, but they are just unsure what to do, what to say, how they can help. One of the things the church can do is to give people the tools so that they can be a help and a support to others in need.

One of the most obvious tools that can be offered is information about who is in need. This information can be shared in a variety of ways – through weekly announcements during church services, through paper prayer lists offered in the bulletin, through phone chains, or electronically through e-mail or other social media. All of these are helpful ways of getting the information out to the people about those who are in need within that community.

One of the most important things to remember about sharing this information is to make sure that those who are in need want this information to be shared. Some people may not want everyone in the church to know about their upcoming surgery or procedure and those wishes must be appreciated and followed. There are many reasons why people may not want their private information shared with the whole church, and this must be respected. I have heard the story of one older woman who did not feel comfortable going back to church after learning that somehow her name had ended up on the Prayer List. I have made it my policy to just simply ask the person if it is okay to include them on the prayer list so others can be praying for them, and respect their privacy if the answer is no.

Once people have the information, then they can respond. Maybe it is by sending a card or note, or maybe by making a phone call. Maybe it is by making a visit. Maybe it is by praying for that person. One of things the church can do is to provide the address and phone number for those in need in an e-mail that is sent or through a paper copy of a prayer list. In doing this the address is provided and people may be more likely to write the card or note than if they had to go and find the address. It is also helpful if the person has made specific requests that these requests be shared. This was the case for a couple from Penningtonville who had experienced the tragic loss of a loved one. They wished for all the prayers and cards, but asked that people not call, as it would be very difficult to talk with people in the wake of such a tragedy.

One of the things that all of us can do is to pray for those we know who are in need. From the stories that people shared, having people praying for them was a very important part of the healing process. Some shared that they could feel that people were praying for them, they could physically feel the support and encouragement that people were offering in their prayers. For some, praying for others is a deliberate and intentional time of prayer, working through a list of people. For others, praying for others happens throughout the day as one's name or situation is brought to mind and a prayer is offered for that person. However it happens, prayer for others is an important way of connecting ourselves to others and supporting them.

Another tool that the church can provide to the people is the opportunity to provide meals to those in need. The church that I serve has many wonderful chefs. After my wife gave birth to our two children, we were treated to the culinary delights of these chefs for two weeks straight. Providing meals is a wonderful way for the people of the church to give of themselves, while also providing a very valuable help to families and individuals in need. At Penningtonville, our Deacons coordinate the meal schedules with those who are willing to cook and those who could use some meals. However, it is important to know the limits of this amazing ministry so as not to overwhelm someone with too much food. Having good communication about what the needs are and how often they could use meals will allow this to be a blessing and not a burden for those in need.

Pastor as Model

One of the most helpful and healthy images of the relationship between a pastor and the church that he or she serves, is that the pastor is helping to lead the church on a journey. The pastor, and the leadership that he or she provides, will certainly help to guide that journey, but the people of the church will also be instrumental in where and how that journey proceeds. The people of a church will watch and learn from how their pastor responds to situations and will often reflect what they see. If a pastor is very negative about the future hope of the church, that negativity will make its way into the people of the church. In the same way, if a pastor is positive and upbeat about the opportunities and possibilities at the church, the people will pick up on that positive spirit, demonstrating it through their own positive actions.

Along this same line of thinking, if the pastor models healthy relationships and connections with the people of the church, other people in the church will see this and pick up on this too. It is important then that the pastor is involved in some of the Community Formation Groups within the church, whether as a leader or as a member. The pastor needs to be a model for the people to follow.

If the pastor preaches and teaches about healing, prays for people's healing, and is involved in Community Formation Groups where significant relationships are formed, then all of that will find its way into the life of the people of the church. Other people will then model this to others in the church, and soon a whole culture of healthy relationships develops to which people can turn in the midst of the struggles, difficulties and losses of life and the church can truly be a place of healing in people's lives.

The Church is the People

The church has been described as the place where one hungry beggar is leading another hungry beggar to get some food. The church doesn't exist for individuals, it is exists for communities – for groups of people to gather to support and encourage one another, for groups of people to learn and grow together, for groups of people to help one another through the healing process. It is the mutual support and encouragement for one another that creates the community environment of a church so that the church can be a place of healing for people. In the next chapter we will look at practices for the whole congregation to be involved with to create that healing place.

Chapter 8 – Practices for the Church: Congregationally

Church as a (W)Hol(l)y Place

There is just something about certain physical places that brings out certain emotions in people. A welcoming playground will bring out joy in little children. The sights and sounds of a baseball park will bring out excitement in the life of a baseball fan. The rows and rows of crosses marking the graves of all the soldiers at Arlington National Cemetery will have the ability to draw out a variety of emotions from different people – sadness, anger, pride, heroism.

The church has this same affect on people. For some, the church is a place of the holy, a place where we encounter God, a place that is set aside, different, special and sacred. For others, the church can be a place of wholeness, a place where people come to be filled up and refreshed and a place where people come to be made whole in their lives. The sight of the stained glass windows, the image of the cross, the rows of pews, the familiarity of the space and many other elements allow the church and the sanctuary in particular to be a holy place, a place of wholeness for their lives.

As we heard from Tim, when he needed a place to go and think through all that was happening with his separation from his wife, there was a comfort in being able to go and sit in the sanctuary of the local Catholic Church that kept its doors open all day long. There was something special about being able to go and sit in the pews where so many other people had sat, and offering up prayers to God in a place where so many others had also offered up their prayers. That was a place of healing for Tim, and the open doors of the sanctuary created that place for healing in Tim's life.

There are of course considerations that a church must think about before just leaving their doors unlocked twenty-four hours a day, seven days a week. Building Maintenance Committees and Trustee Boards will certainly raise questions and have concerns. These should not be overlooked. What should also not be overlooked is the opportunity for healing and wholeness that can be offered to people by having the church doors open all day long, or at least for some portion of the day, maybe over the lunch hour, or for a few hours during the evening. Considerations will need to be given concerning the location of the church in relation to the people who might come to the church, as well as to valuable items that may need to be secured or put away so as not to be stolen by someone taking advantage of the open doors.

The open doors of the sanctuary for regular times of worship also create opportunities for healing and wholeness in people's lives. It is in worship that we encounter God. When we gather with a community of faith in worship, we can recognize that we are there to support and encourage each other. We are not there just to worship for ourselves, but we are there for everyone else who has gathered as well. It is this visible sign of support that can allow the whole congregation to be a support in the healing process. Having this crowd of witnesses surrounding the one who is in need of healing, will give them the knowledge that they are not alone in their struggle or difficulty, but that there are people around them to help in their healing.

Interlude: Mark 11:15-17

> Then they came to the Jerusalem. And Jesus entered the temple and began to drive out those who were buying in the temple, and he overturned the tables of the money changers and the seats of those who sold doves; and he would not allow anyone to carry anything through the temple. He was teaching and saying, "Is it not written, 'My house shall be called a house of prayer for all the nations?' But you have made it a den of robbers. (*NRSV*, Mark 11:15-17)

The Cleansing of the Temple, as this story is often referred to, is a dramatically powerful story, a story that teaches us a lot about how Jesus viewed the temple. The temple was a holy place, a sacred place, a place of prayer. The temple was the place for the people of God to gather and worship God. The chief priests and scribes had turned the temple into something else. They had turned it into a place of commerce, for buying and selling. The chief priests and scribes were trying to make a quick dollar at the temple by selling the animals for sacrifice right at the temple. Jesus was not happy about this, not happy at all.

As Jesus often does when he comes on the scene, he upsets the status quo. Jesus turns the normal and ordinary upside down. Jesus comes along and says, "The temple was not made for this purpose, the temple is a holy place, a place of wholeness. You have set it up as a place to take advantage of people. I am not going to have this." The imagery of Jesus knocking over tables and driving people out of the temple depicts a side of Jesus that we do not often see. And yet, what this story teaches us is the great value and importance that Jesus places on the place of the holy, the sanctuary, the place where the people of God gather to worship.

Worship is an integral part of the healing process, for those who believe in a God who wants his people to be well and whole. Having a place of sanctuary, of calm and peace, a place where we feel we can connect with God is a very meaningful part of the healing process. As we heard in the stories of those who experienced healing in their lives, having a place of sanctuary, a place where they could connect with God and with other people, was a very important part of the process. In this chapter we will look at ways that as a whole congregation we can create an environment of healing for those in need of healing and wholeness in their lives.

Congregational Programs of Support

One way that the whole congregation can be involved in the healing process for people is to be a part of a variety of congregational programs that help in the healing process. These congregational programs can take on many different forms based on the abilities and gifts of those in the congregation.

One of the programs that can be very helpful is to provide meals to those in need. This can be providing meals to someone recently home from the hospital, or to family members who are at home while their loved one is in the hospital. Fellowship meals can also be provided for families after the funeral for a loved one in the church fellowship hall as a way of offering a time to fellowship together. Having different people take turns in providing and serving these meals will allow a greater group of people from the church to be involved and supportive of others within the church.

Another program of congregational support is to send a card shower to those in need.

Everyone in the congregation can be invited to send a card to someone who is coming home from the hospital, so that when they arrive home they will know that there are lots of people sending their well wishes. A card shower can be given to someone in the midst of treatment so that they can know the support and encouragement of their church family. A card shower can also be given to someone who has lost a loved one, so that he or she can feel the support of others around them.

Some churches use a program called Stephen Ministry (www.stephenministires.org), in which individuals are trained to meet and talk with people within their church going through a difficult time or loss in their lives. The great value of this program is that different Stephen Ministers, based on their different gifts and talents, can be paired up with those who are in need of support and encouragement. The Stephen Ministry program also offers great opportunities for training and education in being a true help to those within a congregation.

Congregational Healing Services

For some, the regular worship services of a church can provide a time for healing in their lives. The rhythm of worship, the hymns or songs that are sung, the opportunity to gather with other believers, the opportunity to be in God's presence, these and other elements can allow for healing to occur in some people's lives.

For others, a special healing service may provide this opportunity for healing. Healing services can take on a variety of forms with a variety of elements. A healing service could take place during a part of the regular service of worship, or it could have a time and place separate from the regular worship schedule. Healing services can be specific in nature, dealing with the healing from a specific loss in the community or the world, or more in general based on the needs of those who have gathered.

Most books of worship provided by denominations have at least some basic outlines for healing services. As discussed in the Introduction Epperly (*Healing Worship)* and Evans provide two very good resources when planning healing services. Epperly's book helps the reader to understand the thought behind, and value of, healing worship services in the life of a congregation. Evans' book, on the other hand, compiles many of the healing service outlines presented in a variety of denominational books and hymnals. For anyone looking to start or add to the healing services at a particular church, both of these books will provide great insight and opportunity for the development of healing services.

You Are Not Alone

One of the scariest elements of
experiencing a loss or difficulty in life is feeling that
we are alone in what we are experiencing. One of
the greatest comforts we can have as we begin to
process a loss and start on the road to healing is to
know and feel that we are not alone. To know that
there are other people to support and encourage
us and people who will walk the road with us, will
create a positive and healing environment in the
life of those in need of healing. The whole
congregation can provide this support and
encouragement in a variety of ways, and help in
the healing process. In doing so, the whole church
can portray itself as a place of the "holy and of the
wholly", a place of God and a place where people's
lives can be made whole.

Chapter 9 – Participating in God's Healing Process

Practices in Practice

Sue went to see her pastor after church one Sunday while he was in his office. "Do you believe in dreams?" she asked her pastor. "Yes I do" he replied. "I have had this dream that we need to pray for Jill" Sue responded. Jill had been diagnosed with cancer a few years ago and had been through a long battle with several rounds of chemotherapy and other treatments. Each time Jill went to the doctor to get her levels checked, the anxiety of what the reports would show surfaced again. Sometimes the reports came back okay and other times not so good. Jill however remained positive and upbeat, enjoying the life that she had to live.

"I just feel that we need to lay hands on Jill and pray especially for her" Sue continued on in her conversation with her pastor. Sue had been on the receiving end of lots of prayers and support during her battle with cancer, and she wanted to offer that prayer and support to Jill. Sue's pastor thought this was a great idea and agreed to talk with Jill to see if she would be open to this idea. When the pastor called, Jill was very open to the idea of having people lay hands on her and pray for her. Jill expressed her appreciation for all the prayers that people had prayed for her health.

So on Sunday morning during the prayer time of the service, Sue, Jill and her husband Steve were all invited up front. The pastor explained a little of the connection that Sue felt with Jill and Sue's desire to support and encourage Jill, just as so many others had supported and encouraged Sue in the past. The pastor then invited anyone else to come up and lay hands on Jill and Steve and to join together in praying for them. About half the congregation that day rose from their seats and made their way down the center aisle of the church. With outstretched arms, each one placed their hand on the shoulder of someone in front of them. Surrounded by that group of prayer warriors, the pastor led a prayer.

> God, we come to you today knowing that you are the great physician that has made us and created us. We come to you knowing that you are more powerful and amazing than we could ever imagine. We also come to you knowing that you know more things about us than we could ever know. We come before you today, praying for Jill and Steve. We pray O God, that the cancer in Jill's body would not define who she is. Instead allow her identity as your child, precious and beloved define who she is. We pray O God, for the cancer in her body to be gone, removed from her body. We give you thanks for good doctors and

medical personnel, for chemotherapy and other good medications. And we give you thanks for your love and grace and compassion and goodness that you shower upon us. Protect Jill and Steve. Give them your peace and your comfort and help them to always know that you are right there with them, no matter what the circumstances of life may be. We thank you most of all God, for the love that you share with us through your Son, our Savior, Jesus Christ. It's in his name that we pray, Amen.

After that prayer lots of hugs were given and tears were shared by all those who had come forward to show their support and encouragement. Jill and Steve both expressed their thanks to their pastor. In that moment a bond was forged that will never be broken, a bond between Sue and Jill, who were brought together in that time and place. It is a bond between one woman who sought to be a source of strength and support to another woman who was open to receiving that strength and support. It was an amazing display of one of the practices of the church being put into practice.

Jill will continue to be prayed for by that congregation as well as offered other kinds of support and encouragement. Meals will be delivered, cards will be sent, and calls will be made. That church truly was and continues to be a place of healing in Sue's life and in Jill's life. In that church is a community of believers that truly wants to create a place of healing for people, no matter what struggle, difficulty or diagnosis they face.

What Happens Next?

There is still a lot of uncertainty for what the road ahead looks like for Jill. There is uncertainty for all of us as to where the road of our own lives will lead. There are possibilities and opportunities for all of us. We, however, do not fully know those possibilities and opportunities, nor do we fully know the tragedy that could await us in any given moment. Our lives can literally be changed by just one phone call or e-mail. Our lives can be completely changed by one diagnosis from the doctor. Our lives can be completely turned upside down by just one distracted moment while we are driving.

While we cannot always determine or be in control of the situations and diagnoses that occur in our lives, we can display a great amount of determination and control concerning how we handle what happens in our lives. While there may never be a cure for an illness that has invaded our body, we can determine to live our lives not defined by that illness, but instead to find ways of receiving healing by enjoying and living whatever life we have left to the fullest. While our lives will never be the same after the death of a loved one, we can find healing by remembering the good times spent with that person and allowing their life to live on through our lives. While any loss in our lives may bring sadness and hopelessness, we can find healing in finding new opportunities and possibilities for our lives to flourish.

There is also the possibility for some that even if they receive a cure for their life, they may never experience healing. The deep scars that life has left on someone's soul may just be too deep to ever fully heal. Some have said that with time, the pain subsides, but the loss, difficulty or struggle is never forgotten. It is important for those who find themselves in this stage in life, or for those who seek to be a support and encouragement to someone in this stage in life, to not rush the healing process, to not force healing upon someone. We all respond differently to the experiences of life. The experiences of our lives, whether they were good or bad, will always remain with us. The challenge and opportunity for us is to decide what we will do with those experiences in our life.

Interlude – John 11:1-44

> Now a man named Lazarus was sick. He was from Bethany, the village of Mary and her sister Martha. (This Mary, whose brother Lazarus now lay sick, was the same one who poured perfume on the Lord and

wiped his feet with her hair.) So the sisters sent word to Jesus, "Lord, the one you love is sick." When he heard this, Jesus said, "This sickness will not end in death. No, it is for God's glory so that God's Son may be glorified through it." Now Jesus loved Martha and her sister and Lazarus. So when he heard that Lazarus was sick, he stayed where he was two more days, and then he said to his disciples, "Let us go back to Judea."

"But Rabbi," they said, "a short while ago the Jews there tried to stone you, and yet you are going back?"

Jesus answered, "Are there not twelve hours of daylight? Anyone who walks in the daytime will not stumble, for they see by this world's light. It is when a person walks at night that they stumble, for they have no light." After he had said this, he went on to tell them, "Our friend Lazarus has fallen asleep; but I am going there to wake him up." His disciples replied, "Lord, if he sleeps, he will get better." Jesus had been speaking of his death, but his disciples thought he meant natural sleep. So then he told them plainly, "Lazarus is dead, and for your sake I am glad I was not there, so that you may believe. But let us go to him."

Then Thomas (also known as Didymus) said to the rest of the disciples, "Let us also go, that we may die with him."

On his arrival, Jesus found that Lazarus had already been in the tomb for four days. Now Bethany was less than two miles from Jerusalem, and many Jews had come to Martha and Mary to comfort them in the loss of their brother. When Martha heard that Jesus was coming, she went out to meet him, but Mary stayed at home.

"Lord," Martha said to Jesus, "if you had been here, my brother would not have died. But I know that even now God will give you whatever you ask."

Jesus said to her, "Your brother will rise again."

Martha answered, "I know he will rise again in the resurrection at the last day."

Jesus said to her, "I am the resurrection and the life. The one who believes in me will live, even though they die; and whoever lives by believing in me will never die. Do you believe this?"

"Yes, Lord," she replied, "I believe that you are the Messiah, the Son of God, who is to come into the world."

After she had said this, she went back and called her sister Mary aside. "The Teacher is here," she said, "and is asking for you."

When Mary heard this, she got up quickly

and went to him. Now Jesus had not yet entered the village, but was still at the place where Martha had met him. When the Jews who had been with Mary in the house, comforting her, noticed how quickly she got up and went out, they followed her, supposing she was going to the tomb to mourn there.

When Mary reached the place where Jesus was and saw him, she fell at his feet and said, "Lord, if you had been here, my brother would not have died."

When Jesus saw her weeping, and the Jews who had come along with her also weeping, he was deeply moved in spirit and troubled. "Where have you laid him?" he asked.

"Come and see, Lord," they replied. Jesus wept. Then the Jews said, "See how he loved him!"

But some of them said, "Could not he who opened the eyes of the blind man have kept this man from dying?"

Jesus, once more deeply moved, came to the tomb. It was a cave with a stone laid across the entrance. "Take away the stone," he said.

"But, Lord," said Martha, the sister of the dead man, "by this time there is a bad odor, for he has been there four days."

Then Jesus said, "Did I not tell you that if you believe, you will see the glory of God?"

So they took away the stone. Then Jesus looked up and said, "Father, I thank you that you have heard me. I knew that you always hear me, but I said this for the benefit of the people standing here, that they may believe that you sent me."
When he had said this, Jesus called in a loud voice, "Lazarus, come out!" The dead man came out, his hands and feet wrapped with strips of linen, and a cloth around his face. Jesus said to them, "Take off the grave clothes and let him go. (*NRSV*, John 11:1-44)

The interpretation of this story can go in so many different directions. First, there is Jesus' initial response to stay where he was those additional two days before heading on to be with Mary, Martha and Lazarus. Why did Jesus stay? What was so important that Jesus didn't feel he could leave right there and then? Then there is the somewhat cryptic discussion that Jesus has with his disciples as he is teaching them about walking in the light. Was Jesus just saying that they would be safe to travel during the day or was there more to this discussion that Jesus was having with his disciples?
There is also the proclamation that Jesus makes, that he is "the resurrection and the life" (*NRSV*, John 11:25), a bold and life defining statement that we will not fully understand until

the rest of the story of Jesus' life is lived out. And then of course there is the miraculous raising of Lazarus from the tomb. Lazarus was dead, four days in the tomb, a longer period of time than even Jesus would spend in his tomb. What is most often focused on is the miraculous nature of this story, the miraculous raising of Lazarus from the dead. It is a story of life over death, a story of a cure from death for Lazarus. However, it is worth asking whether this is what Lazarus wanted for his life? Did Lazarus want to be raised from the dead? This would mean he would have to die twice. Did Lazarus find healing in the midst of what took place in his life?

We can only speculate about the answers to these questions, for the healing process, and the process by which we receive a cure are very different for different people. Some may view what happened to Lazarus as getting a second chance at life, while others might be worn down from life and all its stressors, and so ready to move on to their eternal resting place. Just as one person describing the sunset might focus on the magenta haze lighting up the sky, someone else could focus on the fading orange sun, slipping away for another day. Our experiences of healing are very personal and unique, and yet when we allow ourselves to be part of a community that supports and encourages us, those experiences can take on new meanings for our lives and the lives of those around us.

It was not only Lazarus' life that was changed that day. Mary and Martha's lives, as well as that whole group of people who watched and listened as Jesus called Lazarus out of the tomb, were changed as well. Healing changes people's lives. Healing brings us to a new and different place in our lives.

Drawing Conclusions

It is difficult, if not impossible to draw fully complete conclusions about how and what was most effective in helping people experience healing in the lives. Part of this is the idea that has been stated several times previous, that each person will experience the healing process differently. For some people, like Tim going through a separation from his wife, and Mary battling cancer, they did not feel comfortable sharing the details of the difficulties they were struggling through with a whole group of people. Instead, Tim found great healing through the one on one conversations he had with his pastor. For others like Sue who was battling cancer, and Lisa who had just lost her mother, it was the deep and meaningful connection to a small group of people at church that gave them the strength to walk the road toward healing. For others like Jill who we met at the beginning of this chapter who is battling cancer, it was the whole church coming forward to lay hands on her and her husband Steve that brought a touch of healing into her life. For a church to be as effective as it can be in creating a place where healing can happen in people's lives, all three levels (Pastoral, Relational, Congregational) need to be present and working effectively.

There is also no fully accurate prediction of who will receive a healing and or a cure. Medical treatments are still very much a science with a great number of variables that will affect the outcome. Medicines and courses of treatment are prescribed without a complete knowledge of how they will affect the individual receiving them. That was certainly the case for Barbara and her battle with cancer. The doctors felt that Barbara was strong enough for chemotherapy, but in reality her body was much weaker and those last doses of chemotherapy may have actually hastened Barbara's death. Even though Barbara never experienced a cure from the cancer that had invaded her body, she did experience healing, mending the strained relationship she had with her pastor.

Some people will receive healing. Others may experience a cure and healing. Some may never experience a cure but still receive healing. Still others may receive a cure but never find healing. These options all seem so static and separated from each other, whereas in reality I think the lines are much more blurred, with the possibilities and opportunities that each option presents flowing more fluidly in and through the lives of people. It may take years for someone to receive a cure for the affliction that has plagued their body. It also may take years for someone to receive healing from an experience that has scarred them or a relationship that has left them feeling worthless. The word of hope for all is that God wants us to receive healing for our lives. God wants us to be well, and when we are willing to cooperate with God in finding healing, God will be faithful in bringing healing to us.

Where Do You Go From Here?

Healing requires of us some amount of change in our lives, and change is not always easy nor is it always welcome. For some people they would love a change in their lives – a life of less pain, a life of more mobility, a life of fewer headaches – those are some changes some people would welcome. Others though have become comfortable in their lives and so consciously or subconsciously remain where they are, living with the struggles and difficulties of their life, sometimes even relishing in their infirmity. The older woman who feeds off the attention she gets from those who ask her every Sunday at church how she is feeling. The middle aged man whose knees hurt him so badly he can hardly walk some days, but who will not even consider the thought of going to the doctor. The older gentleman who lived a hard life, much by his own decisions, who now in a nursing home never feels the care he receives is adequate without ever being able to express what is lacking.

If God created us, and God loves us, and God desires for us to live fulfilling lives, then God also must want for us to be whole and healthy. This is not to say that there will never be struggles, difficulties and losses in our lives. This is not to say that we will never be afflicted with illness or disease, that our lives will never have any pain. Instead, it is to recognize the place towards which God desires for all of our lives to be directed, a life of wholeness and healing. God's desire for each person that he has created is to live a life of wholeness and healing, whatever that might look like for each person.

The church seems to have lost this message somewhere along the way. In large part it seems that the church has forgotten about the healing ministry that Jesus began and empowered his disciples to continue. Throughout the history of the church and through advancements in medicine and science, the church in large measure has distanced itself from the ideas that healing is possible through our faith and belief in God.

In more recent years, the message of Jesus' healings and the healing power that God offers to make God's people whole and healthy has seen resurgence, as people have been given opportunity to share their stories of healing and others have felt empowered to share their own stories of healing. That is really what this whole project has been about. Listening to the healing stories of others will empower those who have been healed to share their stories, as well as allowing others to see that healing and wholeness is available to them. The church needs to create a space for people to share their stories, and also for the healing message of Jesus to be proclaimed. There are lots of hurting people in our world and the church has a message of wholeness and healing to share, if only there are people who are willing speak this Good News.

How can you participate in the healing ministry of Jesus in your world today? How can you help lead the people you know to receive the healing and wholeness that God has prepared for them? How is God calling you to be his messenger of healing and wholeness? God's healing power is just as real and powerful today as it was when Jesus was walking the earth, healing the people he encountered. The church needs people just like you to proclaim the healing message, to offer the words of hope to the hopeless, to invite people to receive the gift of healing that God has for them. Where is God calling you to be involved in his healing ministry in our world today? How has God gifted and empowered you to bring healing to the people you know and to the world?

Afterword

A Word of Thanks

I would like to take this opportunity to offer my thanks to a whole host of saints who have walked with me and guided me in this process. First, to the amazing congregation of Penningtonville Presbyterian Church (PC(USA)) of Atglen Pennsylvania. They graciously allowed me the time and privilege to pursue the Doctor of Ministry degree at Lancaster Theological Seminary (LTS). I can only hope that they have all experienced and will continue to experience the benefit in the ministry that I provide that completing this degree has afforded me.

I also want to thank my Supervisory Committee comprised of Bruce Epperly, Eric Dreibelbis and Frank Stalfa. Bruce has worked with me on this project even before it truly began in the classes that I took from him during my time of study at LTS. Eric was my resident grammar expert, always making sure my commas were where they were supposed to be. And Frank provided the voice from the other side that pushed the final product of this project to a better place. I am gratefully indebted to Bruce, Eric and Frank for the support and encouragement they each provided during the whole process of researching and writing.

And last but certainly not least, a hearty thank you to my amazing wife Krista, and my tremendous children Owen and Isabel. Many were the nights that Krista put the children to bed alone while I was still at school, and many were the nights when Owen and Isabel would ask "When is Daddy coming home?" Their support of me never wavered and their strength and belief in me spurred me along to completion.

The Healed Writer

Sometimes when a writer sits down to write, he or she thinks they know what they will write or where the text will go. Other times, the writer is more open and allows the text to develop more naturally. My experience was a little of both. The interviews I had conducted provided me the substance of what to write about, the stories that people shared. The question became, how to share those stories in ways that other people would connect to them? How to write about practices of healing in ways that others would see the value of those practices?

What I realized was that the stories that people shared were about real life experiences that all of us may have encountered in our lives. The practices that I proposed were all real life practices, practices that all of us may have participated in our lives. Healing is not something only experienced in the supernatural, only experienced in dramatic and magical ways. Instead, healing is happening all around us, if we are just willing to see and experience that healing.

It is hard to write about stories of healing, without reflecting on one's own life and the healing experienced in that life. I have reflected on stories and experiences in my own life and am able to see a healing thread flowing through my whole life. Healing abounds in our world if again, we are just willing to see and experience that healing.

The healing continues on, in my life, in the lives of those who we have met in this study and in the lives of countless others whom we know and interact with. The healing continues on, as God continues to work through his church and the people of his church to share the Good News of healing for those who are hurting. The healing continues on, as the message of wholeness is shared and those who have been broken by experiences in life, can find that wholeness again. The healing continues on.

Appendix A

Sermon Titles & Scriptures

Mark's Stories of Healing & Wholeness

Mark 1:21-28 - Authority Healing

Mark 1:29-34 - Simple Healing

Mark 1:40-45 - Quiet Healing

Mark 2:1-12 - Vicarious Healing

Mark 2:13-17 - Social Healing

Mark 3:1-6 - Religious Healing

Mark 5:1-20 - Demon Healing

Mark 5:21-43 - Family Healing

Mark 6:30-44 - Hungry Healing

Mark 7:31-37 - Hearing Healing

Mark 9:14-28 - Believing Healing

Mark 10:46-52 - Blind Healing

Mark 12:41-44 - Financial Healing

Mark 14:3-9 - Jesus' Healing

Mark 16:1-8 - Ultimate Healing